William D. Kennedy

Sport, Travel, and Adventure in Newfoundland and the West Indies

William D. Kennedy

Sport, Travel, and Adventure in Newfoundland and the West Indies

ISBN/EAN: 9783337319090

Printed in Europe, USA, Canada, Australia, Japan

Cover: Foto ©Andreas Hilbeck / pixelio.de

More available books at **www.hansebooks.com**

H.M.S. "DRUID"

In the Straits of Belleisle.

SPORT.

TRAVEL, AND ADVENTURE

IN

NEWFOUNDLAND AND THE WEST INDIES

BY

CAPT. W. R. KENNEDY, R.N.

WITH ILLUSTRATIONS BY THE AUTHOR

WILLIAM BLACKWOOD AND SONS
EDINBURGH AND LONDON
MDCCCLXXXV

Dedicated

TO

MY WIFE

WHO HAS ASSISTED ME WITH THE CORRECTION

OF THE PROOF-SHEETS OF

THIS VOLUME.

PREFACE.

THIS narrative of the Druid's commission, extending over three and a half years on the North American and West India stations, was written during the passage home between Bermuda and Devonport. It is a simple record of events which happened whilst the writer was senior officer on the coast of Newfoundland, or cruising in the West Indies.

In the hope that it may amuse and interest my brother officers, and sportsmen generally, I now present it to the public.

W. R. K.

CONTENTS.

CHAP.		PAGE
I.	NEWFOUNDLAND AND ITS FISHING TREATIES,	1
II.	REMARKS ON THE ISLAND,	21
III.	MAGISTERIAL DUTIES,	33
IV.	CRUISE OF 1880,	42
V.	CRUISE OF 1881,	80
VI.	THE ABORIGINES OF NEWFOUNDLAND — THE MICMACS—TRAPPING—GENERAL DESCRIPTION OF GAME BIRDS—ANIMALS AND FISH, ETC.,	111
VII.	THE FAUNA OF NEWFOUNDLAND,	118
VIII.	A DAY AMONGST THE GRILSE,	138
IX.	GROUSE-SHOOTING,	147
X.	THE CARIBOU AND CARIBOU-STALKING,	156
XI.	SECOND EXPEDITION AFTER CARIBOU—1880,	199
XII.	THIRD EXPEDITION AFTER CARIBOU,	219
XIII.	RANDOM NOTES ON SPORT,	239

XIV. BERMUDA, WEST INDIES, AND THE SPANISH MAIN, ... 259

XV. REMARKS UPON THE SOCIAL AND RELIGIOUS INSTITUTIONS OF HAÏTI, ... 343

XVI. A CRUISE AMONGST THE ISLANDS OFF THE MOSQUITO COAST—THE BAY ISLANDS—BELIZE AND GRAND CAYMAN, ... 363

XVII. SECOND VISIT TO HAÏTI, AND CONCLUSION, . 388

LIST OF ILLUSTRATIONS.

	PAGE
H.M.S. DRUID IN THE STRAITS OF BELLEISLE,	*Frontispiece*
H.M.S. DRUID AMONG ICEBERGS,	45
DEVIL'S FIGUREHEAD,	69
EAST BAY—BAY OF DESPAIR,	74
BARRING A RIVER WITH NETS,	130
HALT ON THE PORTAGE—HUMBER RIVER,	171
CAMP ON GRAND POND,	195
BRIGHAM YOUNG,	198
FIGHTING STAGS,	*To face* 230
PADDY AND QUASHI,	238
PORT ROYAL, JAMAICA,	281
PORT AU PRINCE,	325
SAN DOMINGO,	325
CHURCH OF SAN FRANCISCO, SAN DOMINGO,	337
COLUMBUS'S HOUSE, SAN DOMINGO,	338
CATALINA ISLAND,	368
MORGAN'S HEAD,	368
SHEEN CAY, BONACCA ISLAND,	375

SPORT, TRAVEL, AND ADVENTURE.

CHAPTER I.

NEWFOUNDLAND AND ITS FISHING TREATIES.

In February 1879, H.M.S. Druid was commissioned for special service—the protection of the fisheries on the coast of Newfoundland; and in March she sailed for her destination.

Proceeding first to Madeira, and thence to Bermuda and Halifax, she reached St John's, Newfoundland, on the 19th May, announcing her arrival by a salute to the Governor as she steamed between the precipitous cliffs forming the entrance to the port. Before going further, it may be as well to give some idea of the nature of a naval officer's duties on the Newfoundland station, and the reason why the presence of her Majesty's ships is necessary in those waters.

There are many persons living at home who know nothing whatever about Newfoundland; in fact, it is not saying too much to aver that few besides naval officers and a sprinkling of colonial and diplomatic authorities are aware that there is such a place. Some may have heard of it in connection with the dogs of that name; but not one in ten thousand attaches any value to the island, or has any idea of the duties of the ships detailed for the protection of the fisheries, or of the people that fish there, and what they fish for, and what other nations have any fishery rights on its coasts.

I remember, whilst at Bermuda after our first fishery season, going over to call at the regimental mess. A gallant officer was smoking, and we entered into conversation. I happened to remark that I had just come from Newfoundland, and was on my way to the West Indies. "Oh, ah!" said he; "did you touch at St Helena on your way?" "No," I replied, "not this time; but we often do!" With this answer he seemed perfectly satisfied. I mention this anecdote to show how very vague is the general idea as to the locality of the island,—an island, be it observed, identical in size with Ireland or Scotland, and one of the most important, if not the most wealthy, of her Majesty's colonial possessions.

The object of the writer of these pages is to give those who care to peruse them a better idea of Newfoundland, and to enlighten them as to the responsibilities of a naval officer's duties on that station, and as to the importance of the service for which he is detailed.

Some people are under the impression that our difficulties in Newfoundland waters are with our American cousins; but it is not so. It is true that we have had occasional misunderstandings with them, and that paltry squabbles between fishermen have been dignified by the name of "outrage," as in the case at Long Harbour, Fortune Bay—an outrage which cost us the preposterous amount of £15,000, when it is notorious, to those familiar with the circumstances, with the people, and the place, that 15,000 cents would have covered the damage.

But as a rule, we have nothing to complain of as regards the Americans. They come to Newfoundland for bait, and pay in cash; they do good to the poor half-starved natives of the south coast, and are heartily welcome.

It is with the French alone that we have any difficulty; and I have no hesitation in stating my belief, that in no part of the world are our relations with a foreign country so strained as they are in Newfoundland. The position is so anomalous, that any intemperate remark or hasty action on the part of officers of either nation might compromise his Government and bring about very serious results.

The question of treaty rights is a complicated one; it has exercised the minds of many officials, and will probably be a bone of contention for many years to come.

To understand properly the situation, one must go back to the earliest annals of Newfoundland. I will endeavour, as concisely as possible, to put the case before the reader.

Our difficulties with the French began with the discovery of the island in the year 1497; and the value of the fisheries soon attracted the attention of English, French, and Portuguese fishermen. The city of St John's was founded about the year 1578; six years afterwards Sir Humphrey Gilbert took possession of the New Isle in the name of Queen Elizabeth; and in 1621, Lord Baltimore settled the first English colony in the Peninsula of Avalon, on the south-east portion of the island.

Simultaneously with this, the French formed settlements on the west and south coasts, having their capital at Placentia. The whole coast still bears witness to their presence, most of the names of capes, bays, and settlements being either French, or a ridiculous mixture of French and nautical English,— as Rencontre, called Round Counter; Baie-du-Lievre, Bay de Liver; Baie Bois, Bay Bulls, &c.

For the next hundred years there were constant quarrels between the two countries as to ownership, and as late as the year 1713 it was a question whether the island belonged to England or to France, both countries laying claim to it.

In that year England concluded the celebrated Treaty of Utrecht, by the 13th Article of which "the Island of Newfoundland, together with the adjacent islands, were ceded by France to Great Britain in full sovereignty."

The treaty provided that "the subjects of France should be allowed to catch fish, and dry them on the land between Cape Bonavista and Cape Riche." The island was at this time a barren waste, of no value to any one.

In 1763, or fifty years afterwards, these concessions were confirmed by the Treaty of Paris, and the islands of St Pierre and Miguelon, on the south coast of Newfoundland, were ceded to France to serve as a shelter to French fishermen.

These islands are at the present time (1881) occupied by some 4000 French subjects. The harbour of St Pierre is the rendezvous for the French fishing-fleet. This fleet, numbering on an average 100 vessels, assembles at St Pierre about April on arrival, and again in September preparatory to their return to France. They carry from 3000 to 6000 men,[1] who are kept in good order and are under the supervision of the French naval officers. The French attach very

[1] In 1880 they had 6000 men; 1881, only 3000.

great importance to this fleet, as it forms the nursery for their navy. The fishing is heavily subsidised by the Government in consequence, and it is probable that without this subsidy it would have long since ceased to pay its expenses.

By the Treaty of Versailles in 1783, the fishery assigned to the French commenced at Cape St John, on the east coast, and passing by the north, descended by the west coast to Cape Ray.

It will be seen, by looking at the map of Newfoundland, that the island is thus divided diagonally from south-west to north-east, and that the French have the right concurrently to the upper portion of its coast, or about one-third of the whole island. By the terms of the Treaty of Versailles, French fishermen were to enjoy the fishery assigned to them under the Treaty of Utrecht. Unfortunately, the wording of the Treaty is so loose that each nation has put its own interpretation upon it,—the French claiming the exclusive right to the fishery, whilst the British Government maintain the right to be only a concurrent one.

Not only do the French claim the exclusive right to the fishery, but they also claim to have, if not the actual territorial right to that part of the coast where they have the right of fishing, at all events the power to exclude all others from enjoying the benefits to be derived from the land, such as mining, lumbering, and agriculture, so far as the coast is concerned; also, the right to exclude colonial vessels from their own harbours, where they assemble for the purpose of fishing, or for refuge from the weather. Not content with this, they lay claim to the salmon-rivers on that part of the coast between the points indicated, to fish them as they please—*i.e.*, to bar them, regardless of the fact that by so doing the rivers are ruined by exterminating the salmon in the breeding season. In this way several noble salmon-rivers have been utterly ruined. The Ponds river, on the north-west coast, was barred for many years by a Frenchman, who built a dam across it. One year upwards of 500 dead salmon were picked up above the dam. The fish had got over this in some way, probably in a flood, and being unable to return to the sea, had perished. Fortunately, during the winter the ice carried away this obstacle, and it has not since been renewed. One of the finest rivers on the coast, the south-west brook in Hare Bay, was regularly barred by a Frenchman, who set his net across from bank to bank, staked up above high-water mark, so that no fish could possibly ascend: this in defiance of every naval officer who visited the place. This man told me he had already taken 58 barrels of salmon (100 lb. to the barrel), and hoped to take as many again. This was quite early in the season of 1879; and yet a wretched Newfoundlander is punished and his nets confiscated for doing the same thing on a much smaller scale. I have taken many such nets myself, but was unable to touch this one.

The words of Governor Darling in 1856 on this subject are applicable at the present time. He concludes his letter in these terms: "A glance at the map shows the position which this island occupies in the territorial expanse of the British empire, lying considerably nearer to the mother country than any other of her trans-Atlantic possessions — distant only six days' steaming from the British Isles.

"Its shores abound in fine harbours, and its

surrounding seas with the sources of wealth, whilst its inhabitants are a manly and energetic race.

"Yet the political position of a dependency thus favoured is such, that a foreign State enjoys a right to the use of at least one half of its line of coast, and avails itself of the right in such a manner as effectually to close that portion of the coast for all practical purposes against the people of the State to which the soil of the colony belongs."

To go back to the treaties. To prevent disputes between the fishermen of the two nations, the British Government undertook to take the most positive measures for preventing British subjects from interrupting in any manner the fishery of the French during their temporary exercise of it; and in 1786 orders were given to prevent British subjects as far as possible from fishing within the French limits.

In 1788 an Act was passed by the British Parliament empowering the Crown in Council to give orders, if necessary, "to remove all British fishery-works within the French limits;" but this Act was annulled by the war of 1793.

By the Treaty of Paris, 1814, British subjects were excluded from the French limits, as they had been previous to the war; but during the interval between 1793 and 1814, the French having been themselves excluded from the fisheries, many British subjects had settled upon that part of the coast, so that when the French resumed their fishery an entirely new state of things existed—the population had increased and had monopolised the fishing for themselves.

Previous to the war, British cruisers regularly visited the coast of Newfoundland and kept the peace between the fishermen; but after the year 1815, they appear not to have done so until the year 1841, when the French had encroached upon British fishery-ground as far as Belleisle and the coast of Labrador. They were then forced to keep to their own limits.

During this time the Newfoundlanders were never ordered by the Government to remove from French limits, but they were practically excluded by the French from fishing on the north-east part of the island, and on the west were only permitted to do so on sufferance.

Many attempts at negotiation, with a view to

the settlement of this much-vexed French shore question, have been made from time to time, but as yet without any result.

In 1857 a convention was agreed to between the two Governments; but owing to its rejection by the Newfoundlanders, it never became law.

In Paris, in 1860, the Commissioners on both sides agreed to certain articles, which did not, however, meet with the approval of their respective Governments.

In 1866 and 1868 negotiations were again set on foot, but fell through; and in 1875 an attempt was made to come to some understanding on the subject, with a like result.[1]

Any one who has taken the trouble to follow the various treaties bearing on the subject up to this time, can form their own opinion as to the claims of the French to an exclusive right to the fishery between certain limits. That they have strong claims and undoubted rights, there can be no disputing; but that they have an exclusive right, I deny. Unfortunately the

---

[1] Negotiations are now being carried on between the respective Governments, with what result remains to be seen.

wording of the treaty gives them what practically amounts to an exclusive right, inasmuch as " British fishermen are not to obstruct or impede the French on that part of the coast where they have the right to fish, nor by their competition to interfere with or interrupt them on such parts of the coast as they actually occupy and use for the prosecution of the fishery."

What right does that give the French to fish in any river above high-water mark? There is not one word in the treaty giving them such right.

By the wording of the treaties British fishermen have the right to fish *concurrently*[1] with the French, *provided that they do not interfere with them;* but therein lies the difficulty. It is quite impossible, whatever may be said to the contrary, for two people to fish in the same water without one being able to claim, however unjustly, that the other is interfering with him. For instance, a Newfoundlander sets his nets in the open sea; if he catches fish, a Frenchman

[1] See French Dictionary,—concurrent meaning, co-operation, unanimous, agreeing, *qui s'accorde avec;* united—*réuni*.

comes along, sets his net, and says the Newfoundlander is interfering with him. This is constantly done; and as the law now stands, the wretched Newfoundlander, who lives upon the spot, has to make way for the foreigner, who comes out for his own benefit, pays no taxes, and takes away his earnings to his own country.

It is idle to talk about not interfering as the law stands now. The fact is, the letter of the treaty is enforced, whilst the spirit of it is ignored; and it is quite impossible to avoid collisions, which must and will occur between the fishermen of the nations while such an anomalous state of affairs is permitted. Indeed it says much for the Newfoundlanders that very serious outbreaks have not already taken place, as they assuredly will, sooner or later. The Newfoundlander has no choice: he finds himself on the spot, as his parents were before him; he cannot go away, because he has nowhere to go to; he cannot dig the ground and live by agriculture, because he lives upon a rock[1]—besides, the French would object. He must therefore fish to support his family, or starve; and the

[1] The north-east coast is unsuited for agriculture.

French object to his fishing. What is he to do? It is not every one of these poor fellows who can afford to own or charter a schooner and go to the Labrador to fish, as some do.

The French say the Newfoundlander has no business where he is—that he is only allowed to remain on sufferance; but as a matter of fact, the French themselves are answerable for the settlements on that part of the coast. It has been already shown that for twenty-one years—*i.e.*, from 1793 to 1815—whilst we were at war, the French were excluded from the coasts of Newfoundland: it is pity they ever returned! Well, is it likely that during all these years our people were not to be allowed to settle on the coast? that we were to keep the place warm for the French, and hand it over to them directly the war was over? The French came back, found these places settled,—what did they do? Why, so far from wishing to remove the English, they fraternised with them, and encouraged them to remain, appointing them "guardians" of their property during their absence in France, and paying them for so doing on their return.

The north-east and west coasts of Newfoundland now (1880) number 20,000 inhabitants, and these people are expected to exist as best they can. They are not to fish, for fear of interfering with the French; they are not to till the ground near the coast, because the French claim to have the right to prevent them; they are not to mine, because the French claim the strand for half a mile from the beach—by what authority, I have never yet been able to discover.

The Colonial Government, until lately, have not been permitted to appoint magistrates on that part of the coast where the French have the right of fishing, although it is their own country, because the French objected! Consequently these poor wretches, the Newfoundland fishermen, dwell without law, and without doctors except such as a man-of-war can give them.

From May till October this sort of thing goes on; from October till May the country is a frozen zone. The fact is, the wretched Newfoundlanders are slaves, and half-starved ones —oppressed by the peddling storekeepers on the coast, bullied by foreigners, forbidden to catch the fish with which God has provided them in plenty. Even the very naval officers who are sent to protect them are unable to help them; and yet these poor trampled-down folk, who never see a coin of the realm, are told they are British subjects. It's an idle mockery. The treaties are practically obsolete —they belong to a bygone age, and do not apply to present circumstances. They ought to be abolished, or at least replaced by others more suitable to the times.

Moreover, to show to what an extent the French fishery claims have militated against the advancement of the colony, I may mention it was contemplated at one time to build a railway from the capital to St George's Bay, on the west coast; but the project was abandoned, because the French objected to the terminus being at St George's Bay! Again, a valuable silver and lead mine at Port au Port was abandoned for the same cause, although the working of it could in no way interfere with the French fishery operations. For the last few years a lobster-canning establishment at St Barbe's, on the west coast, has been doing a good business, canning 5000 lobsters a-day, and employing some forty men and girls, who would otherwise be destitute. Every year the French have protested against this establishment, although they are not allowed to fish for lobsters themselves; nor does the establishment interfere in any way with the French fishery, seeing that their vessels never go to St Barbe's. Similar protests of this "dog in the manger" kind have been regularly lodged against two other lobster-canning establishments at Port au Port. A copper-mine at Mings Bight, also on the French limits, has been a fruitful cause of complaint for several years past. None of these industries have, however, been suspended, nor are they likely to be so;[1] the French protesting against all such operations on principle—not that they interfere with their fishermen, but on the ground that they have no business to exist! The French know perfectly well that the rigid enforcement of the treaties can never be insisted on, for such an arrangement would be at least as inconvenient to themselves as to us. If such an idea were

---

[1] It is hoped that the negotiations now pending will arrive at a satisfactory arrangement on these points.

contemplated, we should insist on our side that all the fixed establishments belonging to the French on the coast be also removed, and the country restored to its original primitive state. This is, of course, out of the question. Hence each side is, so to speak, winking at infringements on the part of the other.

Much has been said from time to time with regard to the settlement at St George's Bay, which has grown to considerable dimensions. This settlement has sprung up in defiance of numerous proclamations on the part of the British authorities in Newfoundland, and the French say it has no business there. The fishery at St George's is simply a herring-fishery. The French profess to attach great value to it; but as a matter of fact, their vessels seldom go there, as they can get bait in any quantity in the immediate neighbourhood for their fishery at Red Island. It is well known that the settlement is a convenience to them, and they have no wish to disturb it. The same applies to the Bay of Islands and Bonne Bay, which places are seldom visited by French vessels. The poor settlers living in these bays exist solely by the herring-fishery—a failure of which means starvation to them. The French claim that these unfortunates have no business to exist, and that even the lumber trade at the head of the Bay of Islands, forty miles from the sea, is illegal.

True it is that French naval officers are fully alive to the absurdity of these pretensions, which they never seek to enforce; and I willingly bear testimony to the courteous manner in which they invariably carry out their duties. Were it not for that, it would be impossible to avoid frequent collisions: the avoidance of them is only obtained by the tact and temper of the individual officers in carrying out duties which are distasteful in themselves, and in endeavouring to fulfil treaties the terms of which are no longer possible, nor consistent with common-sense.

CHAPTER II.

REMARKS ON THE ISLAND.

THE Island of Newfoundland is, roughly speaking, in the shape of a triangle, each side of which may be considered to be 400 miles long; but this by no means gives an idea of the coast-line, owing to the immense number of bays, creeks, and arms of the sea by which it is intersected. All these shores have to be visited several times during the season; besides which, there are about 1000 miles of the coast of Labrador, also belonging to Newfoundland.

The Canadian boundary of Labrador strikes the salt water at Blanc-Sablon, west of the Straits of Belleisle. To do this work three ships are usually employed: a corvette—the senior officer's ship—a sloop, and a gunboat.

In 1879, the Druid, Plover, and Zephyr were the ships; in 1880, the Druid, Flamingo, and Contest; and in 1881, the Druid, Fantôme, and Contest. These ships assemble at St John's in time for the Queen's birthday; and after a short spell, they disperse on their several cruises, the route for each ship being selected by the senior officer. In August they generally meet at St John's to refit and report progress, and then start on a second cruise, returning finally in October, when they all join the Admiral at Halifax, preparatory to taking their winter's flight to the West Indies. In this way the coast is pretty thoroughly done—each ship visiting the principal places at least twice; but to visit every little harbour and settlement round this extensive beat, would require more ships and more time. As there are but few magistrates or doctors round the coast, or were not up to 1881, the captains and senior lieutenants of her Majesty's ships are sworn in as justices of the peace for the colony, and the ships' surgeons are supplied with drugs and receive a stipend out of the colonial exchequer. In this way the colony gets a good deal of legal and medical work done at a very trifling cost.

I have already, in a little pamphlet published in the colony, described the climate of Newfoundland as second to none in point of salubrity, and I can fancy a smile upon the face of my naval friends at this audacious assertion; but it is a just one nevertheless.

The objection to the climate is, that there is no spring: with one bound the summer is upon one; but that is not till the end of June or beginning of July, although the snow mostly disappears in May. From that time till the middle of October, when the equinoctial gales may be expected, the temperature is delightful, especially on the west coast.

The climate of the interior is altogether different from that on the coast; one has only to go a few miles up any of the numerous fiords which intersect the shores to be aware of this. The north and east coasts are more bleak than the south and west, being exposed to the bitter north-east winds and the full fury of the Atlantic storms; added to which the icebergs are all on this side, being brought down by the arctic current from the north, and are either deflected into the Straits of Belleisle or grounded on the banks—others, meeting the warm waters of the Gulf Stream, are melted, and are returned to the coast in the shape of fog.

Fogs are consequently worse in summer, and the south and south-east coasts are frequently enveloped in them for weeks together, rendering navigation particularly dangerous. Indeed it may be said that whenever the wind blows in towards the land it is sure to bring fog. Sometimes the fog appears in the offing like a wall, when the harbour is perfectly clear; and ships may be seen emerging from the fog, or disappearing into it, in a most mysterious manner. These fogs appear to be cut off at Cape Ray on the west, and Cape Bonavista on the east coast, for they seldom penetrate beyond those points, although one cannot depend on this being the case, as we once very nearly discovered to our cost. In the interior fogs seldom prevail, and do not last long.

It may seem beyond the province of a sailor to offer his opinion on such matters as soil and agriculture, &c., subjects he cannot be expected to know much about; but on the other hand, who is there that does know anything about Newfoundland? The interior is but little known, except to a few enterprising explorers and ardent sportsmen; and in all probability there is hardly a Newfoundlander who has had such opportunities of judging of the capabilities of his country as those whose professional duties have taken them round the coast for three successive seasons, and whose sporting tastes have taken them into the interior as many times.

It is customary to speak of Newfoundland as a barren, rocky, iron-bound coast—and so it is: but strike inland from almost any side or point you may select,—such as Smith Sound, Trinity Bay, Clode Sound, Bonavista Bay, the Gander River, or the valley of the Exploits River, all on the east coast; or the Codroy Valley, the Humber River, Bonne Bay, the Bay of Islands on the west; or in fact along the valley of any river in the island,—and soil of excellent quality, and fine timber in any quantity, will be met with. I speak from experience, having visited all these places. Many of them are uninhabited, and it is a fact that there are no inhabitants at any distance from the coast, except a few settlers on the Codroy and Humber rivers; but whenever, as at these two places, agriculture has been attempted, most excellent results have been obtained.

The interior of the island, with the exception of the high table-land or "barrens," is densely wooded, and only requires clearing and draining to be capable of maintaining a very considerable population.

There are hundreds of fine salmon-rivers in the island, all holding salmon and large trout, besides smaller brooks too numerous to mention; and the coast of Labrador has many noble streams. But I shall have something to say on the subject of sport in another place.

Our first cruise round the island in 1879 lacks any special interest, excepting that it initiated us into the style of work to be done, the dangers to be met with in the shape of fogs, icebergs, currents, and unknown rocks, &c.

Early in the season we visited Rigoulette, a station belonging to the Hudson Bay Company in Hamilton Inlet, coast of Labrador, where the people were reported to be starving.

Sir John Glover, the energetic Governor of the colony, being desirous of judging for himself as to the truth of this statement, embarked in the Druid. We also shipped a cargo of pork and flour for the use of the poor settlers of that lonely and inhospitable region. Having narrowly escaped a sunken rock in the centre of the channel leading to Rigoulette, we anchored off the settlement, and devoted several days to the investigation of the claims, which we found to be based on fact, although the circumstances had been exaggerated. We afterwards visited Cartwright, another settlement of the Hudson Bay Company, and returned to St John's after an absence of ten days.

Sir John Glover, during his term of governorship, made several expeditions into the interior with a laudable desire to acquaint himself by personal observation of the capabilities of the country which he governed; and a large island in Grand Lake is called after him, in remembrance of one of these visits.

The "Truck" System.—Not the least among the grievances of the fishermen is the "truck" or barter system, which prevails in Newfoundland. My first impressions on this subject may be gathered from the following cases, which were brought to my notice. Whilst lying in the harbour of La Poile, a fisherman complained that his boat had been taken from him by one of the so-called "merchants" of that place, in consequence of a claim for goods supplied: the fisherman was thereby prevented from earning his living in the usual way. This happened in the month of May, and he was ordered to attend the Supreme Court held at Channel on the 14th August. The man stated that the claim against him was not a just one, and preferred charges against the merchant. He also stated that he had no means to find his way to Channel, a port some way to the eastward, nor to obtain any legal assistance, and that he despaired of obtaining any redress whatever.

In consequence of this, I summoned the merchant to appear, and inquired into the case, in hopes that some arrangement could be made bearing less harshly upon the fisherman, as it seemed unjust that he should be deprived of his living before ever the case was heard. I found, however, that the order had emanated from the sheriff at Port au Basque, so I was reluctantly prevented from interfering.

This case was but one of many of a similar nature which constantly turned up, and is begotten by the pernicious system pursued along the coast by the merchants,[1] who pay the fishermen in kind in lieu of cash; or if money payment is made, the full value is not given, the fisherman having the option of accepting 16s. or 18s. for £1, or taking goods instead. The result of this plan is, that the men never have any money, and are always in debt.

I conversed with many fishermen along the coast on this subject, and it was always the same story. One man said, "I catch from 200 to 500 lobsters every day, worth 30s. a thousand, and I get in exchange about 10s. worth of goods."

Another said, "This 'truck' system is ruining us, sir; we can never save for our old age, and we are no better off, after forty or fifty years of toil, than when we began." Another told me he earned nominally £150 per annum, and if

---

[1] By the term merchant, I allude to the small merchants or storekeepers along the coast who barter their goods in exchange for fish.

he had the money would do well. An old settler, upwards of sixty years in the colony—a most respectable sober man—assured me that it was with the utmost difficulty he could feed and clothe his family; that he never had any money; and that now, owing to two bad seasons, he was in debt for the first time in his life. They all said, "It is of no use for us poor fishermen to complain: there is no one to take our part." I represented this matter in the proper quarter, but without any result; and I fear it is not likely to be rectified until the fishermen are better educated, and more alive to their own interests. If they could be induced to co-operate together, and purchase their provisions and clothing from respectable houses in St John's, it would be better for them; and I believe that stores on the co-operative system, set up at the principal places along the coast, would be a paying concern.

That this is a grievance of long standing seems very clear—not only from the reports of naval officers, but it is mentioned as far back as the year 1800, in Pedley's history of the colony, wherein it is said: " To remedy this evil will be no easy matter to devise; but one point seems clear, and this is, that unless these poor wretches emigrate, they must starve—for how can it be otherwise while the merchant has the power of setting his own price on the supplies issued to the fishermen, and on the fish which they catch for him? Thus we see a set of unfortunate beings, working like slaves, and hazarding their lives, when, at the expiration of their term, however successful their exertions, they find themselves not only without gain, but so deeply indebted, as forces them to emigrate or drives them to despair." But how can they emigrate? They know not where to go, and have no means if they did know. Born and bred on that barren coast, they know of no other existence; and they live and die hopelessly in debt.

If the Colonial Government were to insist that the fishermen be paid in cash, they would be able to purchase what they want, either on the spot or from St John's, and be able to lay by a little for the winter, when they are unable to work.

Under the "truck" system they are ground down and half starved, having often nothing but corn-cake and molasses to eat in the winter, and not sufficient clothing to enable them to withstand the rigorous climate at that season.

One of the many evils arising from this credit system is the increase of pauperism in the country, entailing a large expenditure from the colonial revenues.

On the part of the merchants it is claimed that they are obliged to charge highly on their goods, on account of the risks they run and bad debts. It would be, consequently, to their interests to pay the men in cash; and I cannot believe they would object to do so. But whether they do so or not, the fisherman is clearly entitled to the money, if he prefers it. An official, paid by the Government, to assist those who are unable to pay for legal advice, would also be a great boon; for what chance does a poor uneducated man stand against one who has means and council at his disposal?

I feel sure that should some remedy in the direction I have suggested be adopted, it would not only be of the greatest blessing to the fishermen, but of permanent advantage to the colony by reason of the additional energy infused into the whole fishing community.

CHAPTER III.

MAGISTERIAL DUTIES.

SOME of the cases referred to us in our magisterial capacity were most amusing. One poor fellow brought his account with the merchant on board to be examined, because he, being unable to read or write, could make nothing of it, nor could he understand how it was he owed the "merchant" sixty dollars, when, by his reckoning, the balance should have been in his favour. A glance at the book showed the delightful simplicity of the transaction. On the one page was credit John —— 60 dols., and on the next, the balance was credit —— & Co. 60 dols. I interviewed that merchant forthwith, and asked him to be good enough to explain the case, as I was ignorant of business matters, and concluded that that was the meaning of book-keeping by *double entry!* He assured me that that was *his* way of doing business. 'I remarked that in England we called it swindling; and so we parted, he apparently hurt that any reflection should be cast upon his character! This individual failed soon afterwards. I fear he was too honest for the times.

A few more cases, taken at random, will show the style of legal (?) knowledge required by the captain of a man-of-war. Whilst fishing in the Forteau river, coast of Labrador, an old settler came up, and after a good deal of circumlocution, informed me that he had a complaint to make against a servant-girl in his employ. At this time I was up to my middle in the river, so he shouted out his grievance from the bank. The stream was swift, and the trout were "on the rise," so the conversation was somewhat disjointed, and occasionally rather mixed.

Mr B. (at the top of his voice). "Serious charge to make, sir. Servant gal——"

"Well, tell us all about it. What's her name? State the case."

" Well, sir, you'd hardly believe it when I tell you that the gal——"

" By Jove, a rise! I have him! Run down and put the net under that fish. Thanks. What a beauty! You were saying that——"

Mr B. " Yes, sir, I was a-going to say that the gal——"

" Ah! another rise. Run down to that stone and you'll get him; a good four-pounder! Go on with the case, Mr B."

" Well, sir, you see the weather is very cold here in the winter-time, and my poor boy is young and innocent like, and——"

" Oh, what a whopper! Quick, Mr B.; take the gaff. Well done! Why, he is the biggest of the lot! You were saying, Mr B., that your boy——"

" Yes, sir, a fine boy; and she wants to swear it on my son, sir: it's shameful."

" So it is, Mr B.; but pressure of business prevents me from investigating the case any further at present—so bring the parties on board the Druid to-morrow morning. Good day."

Accordingly, the next day the whole family

appeared on board—father, mother, two sons, and the defendant, but who, it seemed to me, was in reality the aggrieved party. The case was investigated in my cabin at great length. The woman, who, as they say in the papers, "was of prepossessing appearance," said that she expected one of the brothers to marry her, and she didn't care which! Neither of the brothers seemed to see it, so I settled the matter to the satisfaction of all parties, and they left the ship together. The most amusing part of the story is, that on calling at Forteau the following year, we found the woman duly established in the family, the child adopted, and both brothers willing to marry the girl. So we left them.

A man belonging to Cow Bay complained that his wife, his family, and his feather-bed had been stolen from him, and that on calling for his property he was set upon and beaten by all the party, including his wife and the co-respondent. He considered that he had been hardly used, but said he didn't care so much about the wife and family so long as he got back his feather-bed, upon which he placed great store. I regretted much that the state of the weather prevented me from putting into Cow Bay to investigate this interesting case; but I conveyed to the co-respondent that he ought certainly to give the poor fellow back his bed, and make some small compensation to him for the loss of his wife and children. This, I believe, was done.

The next was a case of arson. A man at Trout river told me that his house had been burnt down, he had reason to believe, by three brothers; but he could not swear to it, not having seen them do it. Summoned all the parties to appear on board the Druid. The three brothers all swore they knew nothing of the transaction. Placed them all under the sentry's charge, while a consultation was held; then called in one, whom we will call A. Worked upon A.'s feelings by informing him that if the case came before the Supreme Court he would probably be hanged; whereupon A. confessed having assisted to set fire to the house. Dismissed A. and put him under the sentry's charge separately, and had in B. Told B. that A. had turned Queen's evidence. B. then confessed. Put him under the sentry's charge, and had in C., who thereupon made a clean breast of it. Ordered the three brothers to pay ten dollars apiece and rebuild the house. All the parties signed a paper agreeing to this decision, and left the ship together. When we came by the next year, all four were living together in the same house in perfect harmony.

I was informed afterwards that in settling this case I had compounded a felony!

The next case was one of forgery, and happened at the Bay of Islands. One man we will call A., was owed by another, B., seventy dollars, and being unable to get the money, had restrained a cargo of lumber belonging to B., and to expedite the payment, forged B.'s name for the amount due. The draft was presented, but not cashed. Each party sued the other, and the case was investigated on the quarter-deck. A. said he didn't know anything about forgery, but that was the way they did business in the Bay.

I compromised the matter by causing A. to deliver up the lumber and consider the debt cancelled, on condition that no further proceedings should be taken by B. for forging his name. The parties shook hands, and left the ship in the same boat. On my reporting this case at St John's, I was threatened with legal proceedings for contempt of court! Nothing, however, came of it. A story was current in the colony of a captain of one of H.M.'s ships, failing to unravel a complicated case where there was a deal of hard swearing on both sides, ordering the parties to appear on board his ship at ten o'clock the next morning, by which time he and his ship were forty miles away! This story, although doubtless a libel, is probably founded on fact.

Many of the cases referred to the captains of H.M.'s ships are disputes about land, and it is not always easy to decide who has the prior claim. I was often engaged a whole day endeavouring to arrive at an amicable understanding. As a matter of fact, we had no power to parcel out the land; but it was better to settle the question one way or the other in the absence of all constituted authority, and I am bound to say that the poor fellows were always satisfied with the decision arrived at on the quarter-deck.

They crowded on board with their complaints, often of a paltry character, but feeling sure of a patient and sympathetic hearing from the "skipper," and knowing that whether they lost or won their case, there were no legal expenses to pay. And I cannot help thinking that the rough-and-ready justice meted out to them on board ship was best suited to their wants; and I have no doubt that if they didn't always get law, they had the benefit of an impartial judge, and generally got common-sense.

Our doctor's experiences were also varied and amusing. People would come on board for medicine, having nothing whatever the matter with them, but merely because it was cheap: one man wanted a bottle of stuff because he had had a cold nine months before! For these simple folk a bottle of distilled water, coloured, and a box of bread-pills, were administered with beneficial results, and they went away happy. The women were always wanting something. As a rule, they suffered from indigestion and dyspepsia, caused by drinking an inordinate quantity of tea, and the men from the abuse of strong tobacco.

Both classes, and especially the women and children, suffer from want of good fare, and often insufficient clothing and hard work. The total absence of milk and vegetables is very conducive to cutaneous diseases, especially when the substitutes are fish, salt pork, and molasses.

CHAPTER IV.

CRUISE OF 1880.

I SHALL now borrow a leaf out of my journal, and ask the reader to accompany me on a cruise round the coast in the Druid, so as to give an idea of the sort of work done by her Majesty's ships whilst circumnavigating the fog-enveloped shores of Newfoundland.

During the seasons of 1879-80 and 1881-82, from May till the middle of October, the Druid and her consorts were constantly engaged on this service. One year's work was very like another, and the places we visited were often the same; nevertheless there may be something of interest to relate in each season's cruise.

I shall now proceed with the cruise of the Druid in 1880.

Left St John's for Harbour Grace. A thriving, pretty town, with clean streets, well laid-out. Several fine brigs belonging to Mr Munn in port, but the schooners of the fishery fleet are all away at the Labrador. Caplin[1] have struck in in large numbers, and are being used for manure.

Trinity Harbour, one of the finest and most picturesque harbours on the coast, capable of containing the whole British navy. The best anchorage is off the town, but there are many others equally secure. On my arrival I found the river in north-west arm completely barred by a mill-dam, thereby preventing salmon and trout ascending. Sent for the owner, who said he was unaware of the law. Told him the law, and communicated with Mr Cole, magistrate, who informed me that there were no less than thirty-six rivers in Trinity Bay barred in like manner. Telegraphed to the Governor and offered to blow up all the mill-dams with torpedoes; also wrote to him officially on the subject. The fishermen complain also that sawdust and rub-

---

[1] A small fish of the herring tribe somewhat larger than sardine.

bish are thrown into the sea from the mill-dams, and that the salmon and herring fishery is destroyed in consequence. There are several clergymen, two magistrates, and a doctor at this place.

Left Trinity June 25th; blowing hard from north, with snow-squalls. Passed Catalina about noon; weather too bad to go in. All the places about here are named by the Spaniards or Portuguese. A dense fog came on at 1 P.M., accompanied by hard squalls and snow; shaped course to pass between Cape Bonavista and Old Harry Rocks, but the current sent us nearly on to Gull Island, which we sighted through the fog when only 300 yards off! Passed through the channel into Bonavista Bay, which we found to be full of field-ice, and an enormous iceberg over 300 feet high. Steamed up to the latter and fired a shell at it. Lay to by the berg till daylight, and then proceeded dead slow, the fog being very thick. Made out Long Island at 6 A.M., and anchored in Goose Bay. This place has never been visited by a man-of-war. The population has increased immensely of late years, and there are now no less than 300

H.M.S. Druid among Icebergs.

families, who live by fishing, lumbering, and agriculture, the soil being very rich. There is no doctor or magistrate, but a clergyman of the Church of England lives at a place called Devil's Hole! across the Bay. Most of the people are away at the Labrador fishing. The river at the head of the south-west arm has been completely ruined by wholesale barring, and the salmon have left in disgust. This year, for the first time, it was not barred, as there was nothing left to catch. Served out the usual proclamations relative to barring rivers and illegal fishing, also that relating to the capture of wolves. Left Goose Arm for Clode Sound at daylight, June 28th: a lovely morning, not a breath of air stirring, not a ripple upon the surface of the water, which reflected all objects like a mirror, the sky included. Shag Island appeared like a lovely gem upon the water. Summer has apparently burst upon us at a bound, and wild strawberries and violets are plentiful along the banks of the rivers. It seems a pity that these fine anchorages are of so little use: they are completely landlocked, and capable of sheltering any number of craft;

the water is always smooth, and the climate quite different from what it is outside, where fogs and icebergs are the prominent features.

We passed the narrows leading into Clode Sound at 8 A.M., after a perfectly smooth and delightful passage round, and anchored off Middle Point. Traversing these beautiful arms of the sea reminds me of the Clyde, but without the villas, or habitations of any kind. The scenery is decidedly pretty, but rather monotonous. Hills of moderate height, densely wooded to their summits, slope back from the banks on either side. There are no inhabitants in Clode Sound—which seems a pity, as the soil is evidently of very fine quality, and the bay is capable of maintaining a large population. Two fine salmon-rivers empty themselves into the bay—one at the south-west, the other at the north-west arm. We followed the former up for five miles, but saw no signs of life, except where some lumberers had been at work, and had stacked some timber ready for shipment. The south-west river is a fine broad stream, but shallow, with no deep pools, as far as we could see. For a wonder, it was not barred; nor did there seem to be any fish in it, as the salmon and sea-trout have not yet struck in. We saw several brace of ducks, but did not molest them, as they were breeding. A settler at Goose Bay told me there were plenty of deer in the winter, and that he had shot fourteen himself. Wild geese are also plentiful at that season. The water is quite fresh in these sounds at the head of the bays. Otters seem plentiful.

June 29th.—Left Clode Sound at daylight for Newman Sound. Another lovely morning, broad daylight at 3 A.M. After threading our way through lovely reaches, anchored at 1 P.M. This place is also uninhabited; it closely resembles Clode Sound in its general features. Two small streams empty into the bay, but at the time of our visit, were worthless for fishing. I am told, however, that when the sea-trout are running, they are full of splendid fish.

June 30th.—Left Newman Sound for Middle Arm; passed between Little Denier and the Brandies Rocks. Salvage is a neat little village, but the harbour is only fit for small craft. A small iceberg was aground on South Shag Island, and several large bergs in sight in the offing. From Cow Head we passed through Bloody Reach,[1] and anchored in Middle Arm at 2 P.M.

This place has not been visited by a man-of-war since H.M.S. Lily was here many years ago. It is similar in every respect to the other fine anchorages in Bonavista Bay. A magnificent salmon-river, the Terra-Nova, delivers itself into the south-west corner of the bay. A few settlers inhabit the banks, earning a precarious living by fishing and lumbering, and in a very small way by tilling the ground. The best anchorage is off the river's mouth, in five fathoms of mud. There are seventeen families in all living in the bay; but the whole of the men, with the exception of two, are away at the Labrador fishery.

July 1st.—A lovely summer's day. Left Middle Arm and proceeded to Freshwater Bay. It is very necessary, in navigating these waters, to travel only by daylight, not only for the safety of the ship, but also on account of the fishing-

---

[1] This name is rather startling, and so is "Damnable Harbour," close by. I conclude the surveyors must have got mixed up, with so many reefs about.

nets which are everywhere set, and would be destroyed by a steamer passing through them, and the poor owners ruined. We anchored at the head of Freshwater Bay at 4 P.M. A fine river, the Gambo Brook, runs into the south-west part of the bay, and another smaller one on the west side. Both of these streams are ruined, so far as the salmon-fishery is concerned, by two sawmills belonging to St John's merchants. The sawdust is thrown on to the bank of the river, and from thence blown into the water, defiling the whole bay. At the spot where I landed, the sawdust was two feet deep, and the bottom was covered with it. The upper mill, $2\frac{1}{2}$ miles from the mouth, bars the river, and the salmon are unable to go up to spawn. Served both mills with the Governor's proclamation.

July 2d.—Arrived at Greenspond at 7.30 P.M.,—a truly miserable-looking place. Several immense icebergs were in sight from the anchorage. The town is built upon a barren rocky island, and although presenting a most uninviting appearance, is a place of considerable importance. It is a favourite resort for sealers and the Labrador fishery fleet when weatherbound. The town contains upwards of 1400 inhabitants, seven-eighths of whom are away at the Labrador. The fishing in the neighbourhood has been a failure so far, owing to the severity of the season. It certainly seems extraordinary that such an unattractive spot should be chosen to build a town, when so many beautiful spots such as those we have lately visited, possessing fine harbours, magnificent rivers, fine timber, and good soil, should be unnoticed and neglected. But the reason is found in the convenience of the port for fishing purposes. It seems a pity that everything should be sacrificed to the everlasting cod-fish, and that the blessings which a bountiful Providence has provided be unappreciated. Better, perhaps, would it be for Newfoundland if the fish deserted these shores, and caused her people to look elsewhere for their living.

July 3d.—Left Greenspond at 7 A.M.; huge icebergs in sight in all directions. The difference in temperature between this place and where we left yesterday is 30°. Here we have it 49°, whilst at Freshwater Bay it was 79°.

The disgusting practice of manuring the ground with fish is carried on at Greenspond to perfection, and to such an extent that these improvident folk often run short of bait, and cannot go fishing in consequence. If, instead of rotting their fields with these useful little fish (the caplin), they preserved them in ice, they would never be short of bait nor of food. The bouquet from Greenspond is so fragrant that we perceived it four miles off. There is now a lighthouse on "Stinking Islands"[1]: certainly the person who named these places had not much poetry in him. Passed numerous icebergs, some of very great size and fantastic form, and arrived at Seldom-come-by at 4 P.M. Thirty-one large icebergs seen to-day. There are 300 people living at Seldom-come-by. No clergyman, doctor, or magistrate.

Sunday, July 4th.—Several people came off to church, and the chaplain afterwards performed service on shore. This place is celebrated for lobsters. A lobster-canning establishment is doing a good business on shore, as many as 4000 being taken in one morning. The anchorage is

[1] Since re-named Cabot.

a very good one—hence the name. Between April 1879 and January 1880, 894 vessels anchored in the bay.

July 5th.—Proceeded up the Gander river, and anchored in three fathoms. The Gander is a noble stream; it drains several large lakes in the interior, and a great deal of lumbering is done, the spars being cut thirty miles up the river and rafted down. A few families reside on the banks, living by salmon-fishing and lumbering. Fortunately the river is too large for barring.

July 6th.—Left the Gander river, and proceeded down the channel between Change and New World Islands,—a most dangerous passage, abounding in reefs and sunken rocks; but that between Fogo and Change Islands is not much better, so there is no choice. Arrived at Toulinguet at 4 P.M. Toulinguet is said to contain 3000 inhabitants, and is the fourth place of importance in Newfoundland.

July 8th.—Left Toulinguet at 9 A.M.; numerous icebergs in sight, and no less than four islands, all named Gull, visible at one time. It is time these places were re-named. At noon we passed close to a very large iceberg over 200 feet high, and of great extent. We carefully tested the temperature, both of the water and the air, when close to it, and found there was *no difference whatever*, although we passed to leeward of it; hence it is quite a delusion to suppose that one gets warning of their proximity by these methods.[1] Entered Hall's Bay at 4 P.M., and anchored near the head about dark. The anchorage is difficult to find, and one must bring-to directly soundings are obtained. The scenery in Hall's Bay is beautiful, but is much spoilt by the forest-fires, which have devastated many square miles of country. Three fine salmon-rivers, all containing salmon and sea-trout, discharge themselves into the bay.

July 14*th.*—Left the anchorage in Hall's Bay,

[1] Possibly notice of the proximity to an iceberg might be given by the thermometer in milder latitudes—for instance, in the Gulf Stream, where icebergs are sometimes met; but in Newfoundland the water is always cold, so no difference is shown. It may not be generally known that icebergs are composed of fresh water, in contradistinction to field-ice, which is frozen salt-water. The former are glaciers which have been formed in the valleys, and have slid down by their own weight into the sea. Seven-eighths of these bergs are below water; they travel very slowly, being unaffected by the wind, and only drift with the current. They frequently ground, and their bulk may be estimated by the mass remaining above water, sometimes 400 feet high and several miles long.

rounded Cape St John's at noon, the southern limit of the French fishing-ground, and anchored in Pacquet Harbour. The head of the bay forms a perfectly landlocked basin, with a pretty trout-stream running into it. The harbour, although confined, is perfectly safe, and affords an admirable opportunity for manœuvring a large ship out of it again. The only settlement is or was in the north-west arm, but the French have now deserted the place.

July 15*th*.—Left Pacquet for Rouge Harbour. Made sail to a fine breeze; passed through a quantity of detached field-ice near the Horse Islands, apparently the remains of an iceberg; also some very large bergs off Canada Bay. Arrived in Rouge Harbour 4 P.M. This is the principal rendezvous of French vessels, and several brigs and barques were lying in the harbour dismantled for the season. These vessels—six in number—carry 60 men each (360 in all), six large boats per ship, besides 60 small boats between them. The large boats are left in Newfoundland during the winter in charge of guardians. The French have done well this year, having averaged 200,000 fish per boat, or 2000 quintals per ship. There are only three English families at Rouge; but at Conche Harbour, separated from Rouge by a narrow peninsula, there are thirty-eight families. They have no doctor or magistrate; one Roman Catholic priest is in charge of the settlement. Many poor people, especially women, came on board to see the doctor. They mostly suffer from dyspepsia, caused by drinking too much tea, and from bad living generally; also other complaints, brought about by hard work and exposure, and insufficient clothing. Settled a case of assault, and investigated several other complaints; which detained me till the 16th, when I proceeded to Croque Harbour. Employed all the afternoon and the next day settling disputes about land and other matters. One family, by name Clanche, very miserably off, in consequence of the idleness and intemperance of the father; sent the poor children some blankets, bread, and meat. Commodore Devarenne arrived in the Clorinde; exchanged salutes and visits, &c.

July 17*th*, 18*th*, *and* 19*th*.—Transacting business with the French commodore relative to the salmon-rivers, the lobster-factory at St Barbe's,

&c. Most of the people on this part of the coast speak French fluently, and seem to like the French well enough. As a matter of fact, they are kindly treated by the French and neglected by their own Government. They have no doctor, clergyman, or magistrate; and except when a man-of-war comes in, they see none of their countrymen. All the trouble on this coast is in the neighbourhood of St Anthony, Mein Bay, and Canada Bay, where quarrels are of constant occurrence. The French have only 3000 men on the coast this year, against 6000 last. This is due to the fact that last season was a bad one, and they had great difficulty in disposing of their fish owing to competition from Iceland, &c. This year they have done well, so perhaps some of the French rooms now unoccupied will be reoccupied next year.

Investigated several complaints against the French, most of them trivial and of long standing. Heard of some difficulties at Ha Ha and Pistolet Bays. These places should be regularly visited, as there are some very troublesome characters there.

July 20*th*.—Sailed from Croque Harbour at 10

A.M. Met the Contest outside; sent her into Croque with complaints against the French in Canada Bay. Made all sail to a fine breeze from the southward; beautiful clear weather, icebergs in every direction. Anchored in south-west arm of Hare Bay at 3 P.M. We have no chart of this fine bay since Cook's survey a hundred years ago; but that is correct, though small. The French have lately surveyed this and Canada Bay, and have charts of both on a large scale, which may be bought for one franc. As soon as we anchored, I went to inspect the southern brook—a fine salmon-river. As I expected, the river was completely barred by an enormous net extending from bank to bank—the lower part weighted by stones, and the upper lifted by stakes, so that not a fish could possibly pass. I told the Frenchman in charge that he had no business there; and that even if he had, his net was illegally set. He merely shrugged his shoulders. Fifty-eight barrels of fine salmon were salted in his hut. Felt so ill at the sight I was obliged to return on board straight.

July 21*st*.—Went up the west brook to see if it was barred also, but found no one living there. The west brook is a fine stream, though not nearly so large as the south-west brook. It is shallow at the mouth, but there are fine deep pools higher up holding salmon and heavy trout. The land hereabouts seems good, with plenty of rich grass and wild flowers. The scenery in Hare Bay is beautiful; numerous pretty islets add greatly to the effect. This bay ought to be called the Bay of Islands—a more appropriate name than its present one. We saw flocks of wild-fowl, and it is evidently a fine sporting country. Sailed for St Anthony on 21st; found there the Flamingo, Contest, and French man-of-war schooner Canadienne. St Anthony is a snug harbour; but great caution is necessary in coming in, as the passage is very narrow, and the harbour is always full of fishing craft. No sooner had we anchored than Robert Simms, chief constable, came off with a host of complaints against the French for taking up English nets and dragging them on shore. At the same time, M. Le Conte, the captain of the Canadienne, came to see me with a heap of counter-charges against the English for interfering with the French. Seeing that affairs were in a very unsatisfactory state, I held a council in my cabin, at which M. Le Conte represented the French, and Simms the English. Between us we drew up a notice which had the effect of pacifying all parties.[1]

July 24*th*.—Left St Anthony for Kirpon. Met with a strong tide-race off Cape Bauld, and several large icebergs in the Straits of Belle-isle. Anchored for the night in Kirpon Harbour, and proceeded the next morning in a dense fog. At 5 P.M. made out the land off Loup Bay, and anchored at Forteau the same evening. Found the current had set us to the north-east two knots an hour. Had we not kept a very sharp look-out both from the deck and the mast-head, we must have come to grief. Oftentimes, when nothing could be seen from deck beyond 100 yards off, the land was visible from the mast-head. By neglecting this precaution a steamer was lost here last winter. An old settler came on board to see me as soon as we had anchored, and in answer to

---

[1] This document was subsequently repudiated by the authorities at St John's, and I was threatened with legal proceedings for promulgating it.

my inquiry how he had got on during the winter, he said—

"Ah, sir, we was on the point of starving, when the Lord God Almighty, who never forgets those who put their trust in Him, in His merciful providence sent us relief! A fine steamer, sir, wrecked quite handy! and loaded with flour, on which we have been living ever since. The Lord be praised for all His mercies." A tear rolled down his furrowed cheek as he delivered himself of this expression; and I fancied I detected a twinkle in the old man's eye as he related with much gusto how they had seen the vessel's mast-heads over the fog as she came on to her destruction, fearful lest she should discover her error in time.

There are twenty families living at Forteau, which is on the Labrador side of the Straits of Belleisle. These poor people have a hard time of it in winter. They have no doctor, parson, or magistrate, and appear to be out of the world, neglected and forgotten. A visit from a man-of-war is looked forward to as a godsend. The bay was alive with fish; but they had no salt to cure them, so had to leave off fishing. Many people came off to see the doctor.

July 29th.—Left Forteau for Lance-Loup, a small port to the eastward, to settle a small matter there between a fisherman and the storekeeper, who is also J.P. The usual thing: fisherman heavily in debt; no means or intention of paying; merchant cuts off his supplies; fisherman starves. I walked across from Forteau with the first lieutenant and doctor, as I wished to examine the lighthouse on Amour Point. The lighthouse-keeper is an intelligent Canadian (all the lighthouses about here are under the Canadian Government). The fog-whistle on Amour Point is placed in the wrong position, and can only be heard when close to; whereas if it was on the Point, instead of round the corner, it would be heard several miles.[1] From Lance-Loup we went, July 29th, to St Barbe's, a very snug anchorage. A Nova Scotian firm have set up a lobster-canning establishment on the Point, at the entrance to the harbour. This has given rise to several pro-

---

[1] I reported this, but the Canadian Government do not concur in my opinion.

tests on the part of the French; but French vessels never come here, and the establishment in no way interferes with them. I went over the factory with the manager. Some forty men and girls are employed cleaning and packing the lobsters, a very interesting process. All the material is made upon the spot, including the tins, and the machinery is of the best description. They often take and tin 4000 lobsters a-day. This industry should be encouraged. There are two small salmon-rivers running into the harbour, both claimed by the French, but fished, and barred, by an old English poacher. They were, of course, clear at the time of our visit.

July 30*th*.—Left St Barbe's for Hawke's Bay, and anchored in the inner anchorage the same evening. On passing Port au Choix we noticed several French vessels in the harbour, but it is too small for us. Four French ships have already sailed for Marseilles with full cargoes. Two fine salmon-rivers in Hawke's Bay are nearly exhausted by many years of abuse, barring, sweeping with nets, &c., till, from yielding eighty barrels of salmon in a season, they now produce only one and a half. All this has been done by two brothers, Eastman, who, having ruined the rivers, have now ruined themselves. The east river has the finest cast for a salmon in the whole of Newfoundland. We only got a few grilse and some large trout.

Aug. 2d.—Left Hawke's Bay for Bonne Bay, and anchored in Indian Cove the same evening. The usual disputes going on about land. The first lieutenant and myself succeeded in arranging matters after two days' argument. Bonne Bay is justly named, being one of the most beautiful bays in the island. It is so large that there are numerous anchorages in it, the best being Indian Cove, suitable for a large ship. Several noble rivers discharge themselves into the various arms of the bay, all holding salmon and fine trout. The scenery is grand, resembling to a very marked degree the Highlands on the west coast of Scotland. There are several settlements in the bay, and the sum-total of the inhabitants makes up nearly 1000 souls. A Church of England clergyman and a Methodist divide the responsibility of looking after them. We remained here five days, our time being occupied in settling disputes of all kinds, but mostly about land. The fact is, that cheap law and cheap medicine are very popular amongst these people, and they prefer to have every paltry squabble settled on the quarter-deck of a man-of-war.

The south arm of the bay extends inland for many miles. The scenery is the finest in the bay, and the soil the richest.

A Canadian settler named Mackenzie has established himself at the head of the arm, and has raised good crops of potatoes and turnips, besides enclosing some land for grazing purposes. He deserves to succeed, but was nearly giving up in despair on account of the wolfish curs which hunt the neighbourhood in regular packs, killing his cattle and sheep; so ferocious are they that he could not send his children to school. I gave him full permission to shoot every dog he could.[1]

Aug. 7th.—Left Bonne Bay at 5 A.M., and arrived at the Bay of Islands at 2 P.M., taking up our old berth in Birchy Cove. The bay

---

[1] I was glad to hear afterwards that he had bagged ninety-two, and was still at it! More power to his elbow!

looks very pretty and thriving at this time of the year: many neat cottages and extensive clearings are to be seen on both sides, giving one the idea that plenty and contentment reign in that peaceful spot; but, alas! it is precisely the reverse. The poor people are in a wretched condition, and would most certainly have starved during the long and severe winter, had it not been for Captain Howarth, R.N.,[1] and Rev. Mr Curling, both of whom, by their noble exertions, staved off this dreadful calamity. Indeed it is notorious that many families are entirely supported during the winter by the latter gentleman, whose life and fortune are devoted to the cause. Should Mr Curling leave the place, these poor people will, I fear, relapse into their former hopeless condition. This year (1880) the fishing has been a good one, so we must hope for better times.[2] The sawmill at the head of the bay is doing a good business, some two million feet of lumber having been cut last fall; and now that the sawdust is burnt

---

[1] Captain Howarth went home on leave in 1879 very ill. He returned to his post, only to die in the winter of 1880.

[2] It turned out a failure after all.

instead of being thrown into the water as heretofore, the herrings are returning to the bay.

Aug. 10th.—Sailed from the Bay of Islands. On passing Red Island I observed the French flag flying from a flagstaff, so landed with the first lieutenant. The *prud'homme*[1] was very civil, and in answer to my questions he said he had hoisted his flag there for six years, and it had never been molested. I thanked him for the compliment of showing his colours to us! and requested him to haul it down, which was immediately done, and begged him never to display it again, as the island belonged to us and not to the French.

Proceeded at 7 P.M., and rounded Cape Ray[2] in a dense fog; heard the fog-horn, but saw nothing. Arrived at La Poile next day. This is a thriving little place, and they have done fairly well fishing. The usual complaint, Fisherman *v.* Merchant; but in this case the fisherman was in the wrong, the merchant having behaved to him with leniency and consideration, which he had returned with impertinence.

[1] *Prud'homme* is the name for the head man in charge.
[2] The western limit of the French fishery.

Aug. 13*th*.—Left La Poile in a thick fog, and reached Little River at 5 P.M. The entrance to this place is only three-quarters of a cable broad,[1] but the water is deep, and there are no dangers, except with a southerly wind and heavy sea, when the sea breaks right across. Once inside, all is calm and peaceful. The scenery is magnificent; precipitous cliffs on either hand, rising to 1000 feet and more. We steamed up into a large basin, four miles from the entrance, to admire the scenery; then turned round and anchored off the settlement. There are nine families living in this secluded spot—seventy souls in all, forty of whom are children. The place is seldom visited by a man-of-war, and they are very glad to see one. The people are very poor, having had a very bad fishing season. Fortunately, game is abundant in the winter.

Left Little River at daylight, August 14th. Stopped off Rencontre to drop the steam-cutter with the doctor, and went on to Hare Bay, a better anchorage. The scenery at Hare Bay is even more remarkable than at Little

---

[1] A cable is 200 yards.

River, although the entrance is not so narrow. On the right-hand side of the entrance approaching from seaward is a remarkable rock bearing the likeness to a man's face. It is called, out of compliment, the "Devil's Figurehead." I consider Hare Bay to be the finest scenery in Newfoundland, reminding one of a fiord in Norway. There is a beautiful site for a settlement at the head of the bay, with a fine salmon-river close at hand, and a gentle slope to the barrens at the back, whereon deer, bear, and grouse are to be found. We saw two bears, and killed some grouse. The sole attraction — cod-fish — is alone wanting; hence the reason why Hare Bay remains uninhabited, and happily undefiled by putrid cods' heads, the main feature in the other settlements round the coast.

Devil's Figurehead.

Sunday, Aug. 15th.—Left Hare Bay for Salmonier. The greatest caution is necessary in approaching the islands of St Pierre and Migelon, especially in foggy weather, as it generally is, on account of the strong currents which prevail in that neighbourhood. We shaped a course to pass between Migelon and the Seal Islands, and yet passed outside the latter.

Arrived at Salmonier August 16th. This place is steadily improving, and will one day be of great importance. It may be called the Brighton of St John's, and when the railway is completed, will no doubt become a fashionable watering-place.

We noticed a good deal more land cleared since our last visit in 1879, and some thriving crops on the hillsides. A trip up the Salmonier river at this season of the year will well repay one. The scenery is beautiful, and the accommodation at Carew's Hotel is good of its kind.

In consequence of a telegram from the Governor, I put to sea on the 19th August at 9 P.M., and went to the assistance of the steamer Flavian, ashore at Great Island, on the south-east coast. We rounded Cape Race, as usual, in a dense fog, and arrived off Great Island at noon next day. The Flavian was hard and fast in a cove, with the sea breaking all round. After considerable trouble and no little risk, we got hold of her with our wire hawsers, but could make no impression upon her, although the engines were working at full power; so we went on to St John's for further assistance. On the 22d and 23d we again went down to the Flavian, but with the same result. To make a long story short, we made no less than five attempts to tow the vessel off; finally, on 10th September, after she had been ashore twenty-nine days, and had 3000 tons of cargo taken out of her, she floated just as we were getting our hawsers fast to her for the last time. That a ship should be on the rocks on this iron-bound coast for a month, and finally get off, is one of the most extraordinary events that ever happened. It may be attributed in a measure to the fact that the ship was brand-new, on her first voyage, and very strongly built. The means taken to lift her by pontoons, &c., were most interesting, but would make too long a story to relate here. The Druid was twice in a most perilous position herself during these operations, owing to the heavy sea beating on the weather shore of the island, where the Flavian was. Officers and men worked with a will; but although the captain, and Lloyd's agent, who came out from England to assist in the operations, expressed their gratitude for our endeavours in the highest terms, not one word of thanks or notice of any kind did we ever get from the owners.

On 12th September, two days after the Flavian floated, we were off again on a second cruise, and reached Trepassey Harbour the same night. The next morning off again at daylight for St Mary's, and from thence to Great St Lawrence. Thick fog and rain all day; nevertheless we made the harbour's mouth exactly. We find the safest way in a fog is to stand boldly in for the shore, keeping a very sharp look-out from all parts of the ship. The breakers will always be seen at from 150 to 200 yards off; but with the engines under command, there is not much risk, and the entrance can generally be made out. The lead is of little use, as the water is usually deep right alongside the rocks. I have tried sending boats ahead again and again, and generally found that the boats have lost their way, and we have got in without them. We found that the reverberation of the fog-whistle from the cliffs was also a sure guide as to their distance.

Anyhow, it is nasty work groping about in a fog, with wind and sea setting on shore, and no anchorage. If you stand off, you may wait for weeks for the fog to lift, and get drifted about by currents, till you cannot tell where you are.

Sept. 16th.—Detained in Great St Lawrence by dense fog. On 17th it lifted, and we got out and proceeded round to St Pierre. I was desirous of ascertaining if they had any guns mounted in St Pierre; so we saluted the French flag with twenty-one guns, which was immediately returned.

There are between 4000 and 5000 inhabitants in the place, besides a floating population of some 2000 more who return to France at the close of the season.

A considerable trade is carried on with Canada and Nova Scotia, and a good deal of smuggling with the southern ports of Newfoundland. The island is connected by cable with France, England, Newfoundland, and Nova Scotia.

Sept. 18*th*.—Sailed for the Bay of Despair—or Des Espoirs, according to the French charts. Some hours afterwards we observed a schooner flying a signal of distress. She proved to be the Obeline, of and from the Gut of Canso, laden with cattle and sheep for St Pierre. They had been nineteen days at sea. The master had no idea where he was, and the cattle were starving.

East Bay—Bay of Despair.

Took the craft in tow, and proceeded up the north-east arm of the Bay of Despair. Scenery magnificent, and weather perfect. After forty miles of this inland navigation, we anchored in Ship Cove—a very snug little place. No man-of-war had been here for three years. There are eleven families in the Cove. They live by cultivating the land and raising cattle. They do but little fishing, being so far from the sea; but they carry on a little trade with St Pierre—making hoops for casks, and bringing back general cargoes in return. They have no doctor or priest, and say they get on very well without them. An old couple named Collier number ninety and ninety-five years respectively—which speaks well for the climate. There are several settlements scattered about in the neighbouring creeks and arms of the bay, and an Indian encampment in Conne River. A fine salmon-river runs into the head of the main branch, and a telegraph station[1] beside it. Altogether, this is an interesting place. These primitive folk lead quiet, uneventful lives: they are pretty well independent of the truck system, at peace with all the world, and seemingly indifferent to what goes on in it—beyond their bay. Plenty of grouse are to be found on the barrens in this neighbourhood, and deer in the winter. After a couple of days spent pleasantly here, we put

---

[1] I have frequently mentioned the telegraph station at out-of-the-way and sometimes uninhabited places along the coast. These stations are for the purpose of keeping the line in working order. A repairer lives there, and is responsible for the condition of the line for several miles on each side of the station.

to sea, towing the Obeline, which we cast off outside, with a fair wind, for St Pierre. Anchored in Hare Bay the same afternoon.

Sept. 23*d.*—Proceeded on to White Bear Bay, to communicate with the telegraph station at the head. This is a fine bay, twenty miles deep, with a good anchorage at the head. The only living creatures are the operator and his family, and one telegraph repairer![1] Truly a lonely life. Game is plentiful in winter—deer, bears, and ptarmigan in abundance. From White Bear Bay we proceeded once more to visit our friends at the Bay of Islands, anchoring on this occasion at Petipas Cove, the best anchorage. We found the poor people in great distress, owing to the failure of the herring-fishery; and they have no other means of earning a living. Mr Curling supports many families out of his private purse; but it is not fair that he should support the whole population of the bay.

The people on the west coast have no rep-

---

[1] In the winter-time the repairer has very hard work, as the wires are often broken down by snow and the posts levelled by gales. They have to travel long distances in sleighs drawn by dogs, and are frequently away for days together.

resentative in the local Parliament; and yet they are taxed, without reaping any advantage.[1] They have no roads worthy the name, and no schools—the money voted for the former being all swallowed up in providing for the paupers. A little encouragement from the Government is needed to develop the resources of this part of the coast. There is plenty of wealth in the country. Coal, marble, silver, lead, and asbestos have been found; but this part of the island is paralysed by the dread of French occupation, however unfounded. There is hardly a respectable merchant on the west coast; and no one can be found to settle without some guarantee that he will not be molested by the French, who claim to have the right and the power to turn him out at any moment. This, of course, they cannot do; but still the feeling of insecurity exists, and everything remains *in statu quo*.

Oct. 2d.—Proceeded to York Harbour. There are only two huts here, and the poor people are in a sad state of destitution, having actually no means of living, now that the herring-fishing has failed. The doctor's visit was opportune;

---

[1] I hope and believe this has now been rectified.

but what they require is food, not physic. On the 9th October the ship proceeded to Lark Harbour, where there are eight families—about forty people—in the same sad state of destitution as in other parts of the bay.

Oct. 11th.—Returned to Petipas Cove. Many people came off to see the doctor. There is now no doctor or magistrate in the bay, and the people are too poor to pay for a medical man. This destitution is sad to behold, and there seems no remedy for it. Our visit is looked forward to as a godsend, for the money spent by the ship is a great help, and the poor people feel they are not altogether abandoned or forgotten in the world. We left the Bay of Islands finally on 13th October, and after coaling at Sydney, Cape Breton, returned to St John's on the 18th, and soon afterwards joined the Admiral at Halifax.

The above description, which I have copied word for word from my fishery journal, will give to any one who has taken the trouble to follow the somewhat monotonous daily routine, a fair idea of the duties of one of her Majesty's ships on the fisheries. That it is not altogether a bed of roses must be evident to the reader, when all the risks and anxieties incidental to the navigation of these coasts is considered. The constant fogs, variable and strong currents, hidden rocks, and abundance of field-ice and icebergs, are a fruitful source of danger to the mariner. On the other hand, the work is most interesting in a diplomatic sense—and when the weather is fine the cruise partakes of yachting; added to which, one has the satisfaction of feeling that one is doing good work in visiting these out-of-the-way places, and in looking up the poor neglected folk who inhabit them. To a sportsman, there is also an abundant field for amusement, either with rod, gun, or rifle, when time permits; and above all this, the glorious independence of the life is to me its greatest charm.

CHAPTER V.

CRUISE OF 1881.

I DO not propose to follow the ship from place to place during the season of 1881, as in the previous year, because many of the places visited were the same as the year before, and it would be a useless repetition; but on the other hand, there are several places which we had never visited either in 1879 or 1880. I shall have a few remarks to make *apropos* of them. Some of these had never been visited by a man-of-war in the memory of the oldest inhabitant, and were not even surveyed. This season we were hurried up from the West Indies a month earlier than usual, at the request of the Governor, who feared another outbreak in Fortune Bay. That this alarm was a visionary one I will presently show. Anyhow, we left Halifax for Fortune Bay on the 21st April, and two days afterwards found ourselves beset with field-ice coming out of the Gulf of St Lawrence, and apparently extending from the shores of Cape Breton Island to the south-west coast of Newfoundland. A small detour in our course enabled us to avoid this obstacle; and after touching at St Pierre, where several French merchant-vessels had already arrived, we entered Fortune Bay on 25th April—the time appointed by the Admiral. There are several good harbours in this fine bay, notably Harbour Briton, St Jaques, and Belloram, all of which we visited. At all of these places there are magistrates; and these gentlemen, one and all, ridiculed the idea of a disturbance at this time of the year.

In January the herrings congregate in Long Harbour by myriads, and it is at that time that a disturbance is more probable; although, as a matter of fact, with the exception of the one which caused so much excitement in January 1878, no collision has ever occurred either before or since.

F

Belloram is a snug little place and a thriving settlement. There are 140 families living in the bay, numbering 500 inhabitants. Mr Bishop,[1] the clergyman, has lived at Belloram for thirteen years; he has never known a man-of-war come into the bay. The people are very orderly, and not a single serious offence has been committed during the whole of that time : what place could say the same? On the 27th April we entered Long Harbour and anchored near the head, some fifteen miles from the sea. The so-called "Fortune Bay outrage" occurred at a place called the "Tickle Beach," about four miles from the entrance. We stopped there for a short time to communicate; but there was only one man there, and the anchorage is a bad one, so we did not remain. There is a telegraph station at the head of Long Harbour, seven miles above the anchorage; and a fine salmon-river, with good grouse-ground on the barrens on both sides. Deer, ptarmigan, and wild geese are plentiful. Altogether it is a most sporting-looking country, and quite undisturbed.

There being nothing to detain us in Long

---

[1] Since dead.

Harbour, we continued our rounds, visiting St Lawrence, Placentia, and Burin. The two last-named places we had never been to before; both are of considerable size, and well worth a visit. There are 3500 inhabitants at Burin, with a magistrate, clergyman, and doctor. The harbour is excellent, snug, and very picturesque.

Placentia has about 1000 inhabitants; it was formerly the French capital. There is also a magistrate, doctor, and Roman Catholic priest. The anchorage is only a fair one, being open to the south-west; but the holding-ground is good.

From Placentia we touched at Salmonier, St Mary's, and Trepassey, and arrived at St John's May 16th, about the usual time for ships to reach St John's from the West Indies, without this preliminary canter.

After a short spell for rest and refreshment, and having been joined by my colleagues, we dispersed again on our several cruises, the Fantôme taking the southern route, whilst we went up the east coast. Our first port of call was Harbour Grace, and from thence to Heart's Content,—pretty names both of them. The latter is the terminus of the Atlantic cable, and, as a harbour, is second to none in Newfoundland, or, for the matter of that, in any country. There are about 1200 inhabitants in the town. Mr Murray, the rector, showed us with pride the beautiful church he was building—the cost being defrayed by voluntary subscriptions, I believe. We then stood across Conception Bay to Smith's Sound, and anchored near the head. Smith's Sound is fairly populated—several small settlements being scattered on both sides of it. The soil is good, and attempts have been made to cultivate it. Several small rivers discharge themselves into the bay; but as these have all been barred for twenty years, no salmon can ascend them. As I reported this circumstance last year, and no notice was taken of it, I left the dams unmolested, merely recommending the owners to make salmon-ladders in the middle, which they promised to do, but are not the least likely to perform. I conclude the authorities consider the lumber trade to be more profitable and important than the salmon-fishery; if so, it is no business of mine. All I know is, that the lumber trade is declining all over the country, and at the present rate of forest-fires will soon be a thing of the past; whereas the salmon, if properly protected, last for ever.

Rabbits are so numerous that one old settler told me that he and his two children had shot or trapped 500 dozen in two seasons, selling the skins for 1d. each. The scenery in Smith's Sound is pretty enough, but bears no sort of comparison with that on the south coast, such as Hare Bay, Little River, and the Bay of Despair.

From this place we called at Trinity, and from thence pushed on for Toulinguet. On approaching Toulinguet we found an immense field of ice, extending to the northward as far as the eye could reach—necessitating a long detour, unless we could force a lane through it, which we proceeded to do. Selecting a weak spot in the icy barrier, we put the old Druid at it. The first shock brought her up all standing, like a billiard-ball; but recovering her previous momentum, she gradually bore through, with no further damage than the loss of a few sheets of copper from her stem. This field-ice is very treacherous—it looks so broken and easy to get through; but when it is considered that seven-eighths of the bulk are below water, it can be easily understood that blocks as big as the quarter-deck, *above water*, offer considerable opposition to the passage of a ship. It must also be borne in mind that if one cannot get through, it is also impossible to turn round, and difficult to back out, without risking the loss of, or damage to, the propeller. Toulinguet is a pretty place, and an excellent and capacious anchorage; it is a favourite rendezvous for the Labrador fishing fleet.

Whilst steaming up the Exploits river a day or two afterwards, we noticed a strong smell of burning, with a thick smoke extending many miles to seaward, caused by an extensive forest-fire on the mainland. The sun was partially obscured the whole day, glowing through the smoke like a red-hot shot, and casting a lurid glare upon the water quite beautiful to behold. The atmosphere became close and stifling as we ascended the river, the thermometer showing 79° against 40° outside. The temperature of the water also rose from 35° to 50°. On coming to an anchor at 4 P.M., we learnt that a fire had been raging for weeks, and the people feared it must have reached the settlement at Hall's Bay, and the mine at Little Bay.

Soon after we had anchored, the "oldest inhabitant" came on board to see me. I gave him a good stiff glass of old Scotch whisky, which loosened his tongue.

"Them's fine heads," said he, looking at my caribou heads in the cabin; "but Lor', sir, they're nothing to some I shot when I first came here." Whereupon he related the following story:—

"I was a-beating up the river some years ago, when I seed, as I thought, a tree floating down. But I soon saw they was two fine stags; so I puts me 'elm down, and seizing my gun, I shoots 'em, right and left: and would you believe me, the horns of one was 5 feet $11\frac{3}{4}$ inches across, and the other over 6 feet!"

Later in the evening, after more grog, he related the same yarn; but the horns had grown considerably, until, just as he was going away, I asked him particularly what the dimensions of those horns were.

"Well, as far as I can remember, captain, one

was just 9 feet 4½ inches, and the other nearly 11½ feet!"

The next morning, June 16th, a party of officers and myself, taking advantage of a short spell that our poor worn-out engines required, started up the river in the steam-cutter to visit the Grand Falls, which few white men have seen. The same afternoon we reached a desirable camping-ground, twelve miles from the ship, and about two from the Bishop's Fall. The scenery on the Exploits is monotonous, and not remarkable at first. The river is a very fine one, about a mile broad at the mouth. It gradually narrows to half a mile, which it maintains for ten miles. The banks are well timbered, but most of the best pine-trees have been already cut down. Bishop's Fall is formed by a succession of cascades, and presents a fine appearance. The total height is about 20 feet. Above the Fall is a long "steady" or stretch of smooth water for several miles, till the Great Rattling Brook, a tributary to the main stream, is reached, after which rapids again commence. We fished below the Falls without success, for we were too early for the salmon. The rocks forming the

Fall are heavily scored by ice, and are as smooth and slippery as glass. Whilst examining them I came across a young seal. The young rascal showed his teeth, so I killed him with a stone, and kept his skin. This kind of seal whelps in the fresh water, and does not, I imagine, descend to the sea; at least we met with many seals the next day, with their cubs, several miles up the river. Returning to our camp, we found the tent pitched, fire lighted, and tea ready, and we looked forward to refreshment and repose; but alas! there was none of it, for the black flies were masters of the situation. They were in millions, and attacked us from all quarters, notwithstanding repeated applications of tar and oil, until we had to take refuge in the smoke of our fire, where we passed a miserable time, with our eyes running with water, mingled with grease and tar. We endeavoured in vain to make ourselves comfortable for the night; but the flies got into our eyes, ears, and mouth, mingled with our food and tea, and generally made our lives a burden to us. Darkness set in, and we flattered ourselves we should have peace; but there was no peace for the wicked.

The flies disappeared, but the mosquitoes took their place. The tent was stiflingly hot, and we tried to sleep outside; but it was all the same, for no sleep was to be had, and muttered but very excusable curses might be heard from some poor sufferer the whole night long. It has always been a wonder to me what these brutes are put into the world for, and why they cannot be satisfied with taking one's blood, to which they are heartily welcome, without poisoning one also: it's one of those things no fellow can understand.

With early dawn we were all astir, and after a refreshing plunge in the river, and a cup of coffee, Cochrane and I started in a canoe to explore the river, and, if possible, reach the Grand Falls. Some of the youthful members of our party undertook to bathe, to the horror and amazement of a worthy settler, who had accompanied us in the capacity of pilot for the river, and who boasted that he had been thirty years in the country without washing.

To follow the canoe: we carried her over the rocks and launched her on the waters above the Bishop's Fall, and sometimes paddling, sometimes walking for eight miles, reached the Great Rattling Brook, where we stopped to lunch and fish. This is a fine salmon-river, but there were no fish in it at that time. The Indians showed us the pool where they speared the salmon in the breeding season; but that was all the satisfaction we got, so we crossed the main river and landed on the opposite shore to walk to the Falls, as the Indians said the rapids were too strong to pole against. The bank was sloping and rocky, and covered with bush, so that it took us three weary hours to reach the rapids, from which a trail led through the woods to the Grand Falls. Numerous seals reposed upon the rocks or disported themselves in the whirling rapids, shouting to each other with notes of alarm at our approach: the fond mothers were generally accompanied by their young, whom they tenderly guarded. The river at this place took a sharp bend to the right, and the scenery at once became more weird and grand. Following the trail through the woods, we now approached the Grand Falls, the roar of which we could plainly hear. Occasional glimpses of the river far beneath us could be had through the trees, showing a mass of foaming, eddying water dashing between precipitous banks on either hand. Guided by the ear, we now scrambled through the bush, and presently found ourselves in sight of the Falls, when a glorious view presented itself. I must confess that we were prepared for a disappointment, after many of like nature in this and other countries; but the scene before us fully answered, if it did not exceed, our expectations. Looking upwards to the right was a roaring torrent broken by the black rocks, whose heads could now and then be seen. Abreast of where we stood the stream was divided by a thickly wooded islet, whereon thousands of gulls had built their nests; the parent birds flew round with loud discordant cries, adding in the roar of the waterfall to the weirdness of the scene. Below the islet the waters met, and, wedged in by precipitous rocks on either side, plunged in a succession of cascades into the seething caldron beneath.

Seating ourselves beside the fall, we contemplated this fine sight—not a soul to interfere with us. Here were no touting loafers to offer to "take you under the Falls for half a dollar," as at Niagara; no quack advertisements defacing the rocks, as may be seen on the Hudson river: all remained as God made it. Long may it be so.

Possibly with the completion of the railway we shall have a station at Exploits river, with a hotel at the Grand Falls; but in the meantime, let us rest content that we have seen, without question, the finest sight in Newfoundland, untouched by the hand of man. It has been the privilege of but few white men to have seen these Falls, and only one of our Indians had seen them before. A very fine view must be obtained both from above and below the Falls, but the limited time at our disposal prevented our doing more than resting for a short half-hour on the spray-covered rocks, and taking a rough sketch of the scene, before starting on our wearisome walk back.

The whole height of the Falls is given at 145 feet, but of this a good deal is broken water. I should estimate the largest fall at not more than 50 feet, and perhaps as many across the gorge. But the beauty of the Falls is not so much in their height as in the immense body of water compressed into this space, and in the general wildness of the place. Our trudge back was not pleasant nor interesting to relate: walking on the side of one's foot, with one leg in the water, climbing over boulders and snags, for seven hours, with no food or whisky left, gets monotonous, and glad were we to find ourselves gliding down-stream and shooting rapids in a birch-bark canoe; and dreading another night with the mosquitoes, we reached the ship the same night.

There is, in my humble opinion, much valuable land on the banks of the Exploits capable of cultivation and of supporting a considerable population; it seems a pity it is not more settled. The climate is mild as compared with the seacoast. The sons of fishermen might be encouraged to settle and cultivate the land, instead of following the precarious living adopted by their parents. Now that the fisheries are unquestionably insufficient to maintain an increasing population, this becomes every day a more important question. Besides, the men need not give up altogether their beloved fishing; they might still prosecute the Labrador fishery, returning to their homes by the river in the fall of the year. Some very fine craft, suitable for this trade, are built upon the Exploits. But before settling in this part of the country, it is absolutely necessary to clear away the timber in the vicinity of a settlement to secure one's self against forest-fires, and to get rid of the flies and mosquitoes, both of which interfere greatly with a settler's comfort and prospects, and are only too common on the Exploits river. By clearing away the woods round about his house, a man at once places himself in safety as regards fire, and the flies disappear to a great extent, as may be seen at Messrs Vallance & Winsor's sawmill at the mouth of the river. The first objection—that of fires—will probably right itself shortly; for, at the present rate of fires, there won't be much more timber left to burn. As for the flies, it would be simply impossible for any one to settle on the banks of that or any other river in the island, with any degree of comfort, unless the bush be first cleared away. Some of the old settlers of thirty and forty years' standing told us that they were bitten just as badly as when they first came into the country, and their bleeding hands and faces testified to the fact. The wretched women and children could not leave their houses to work in the garden unless it was blowing a gale or raining in torrents; and these pests last from June till October, the best months in the year.

June 18*th*.—Proceeded to Hall Bay. Found a forest-fire had been burning for more than a week, devastating an immense tract of country, and leaving many poor families destitute and quite homeless. It was indeed sad to see so many poor women and children who had lost everything they possessed, and yet to be able to do so little for them. However, we were able to be of some assistance, and our opportune arrival cheered the poor things up. Many came on board for a little assistance. We also sent six carpenters and twelve blue-jackets to assist in rebuilding their houses for them. Fortunately the saw-mill had escaped, so lumber was plentiful, and our fellows soon had the frames of several houses up. Providentially no lives were lost, but some families had a narrow escape. All the men were away up the river lumbering when the fire broke out, and the women had to do all the work, and had enough to do to save their children. Consequently all the personal effects of the unfortunate lumberers were lost, many having nothing in the world but what they stood up in. Most of these lumberers are Canadians. They all say that the lumber trade is declining, that the country is a hard one to get a living in, and they talk of returning to their native land as soon as possible.

The whole country on the north bank of Indian Brook is now burnt, presenting a most desolate appearance, and the beauty of that picturesque stream has departed — never to return.

The site for the terminus of the proposed railway is at the head of Hall's Bay, between the south and west brooks; and should the railway be ever carried thus far, this place will become of great importance. The anchorages are not first-rate, but that at the head of the bay is safe, and there is deep water close to the shore, so that the largest ships could lie alongside the wharfs, which would be built for the shipment of copper-ore, &c., as at Little Bay and other places along the coast.

June 23*d.*—We left Hall's Bay, where our presence has been a perfect godsend, and proceeded to Little Bay Mine, a wonderfully snug little port, perfectly landlocked and sheltered from all winds. Large vessels can lie alongside the pier, and two fine steamers were loading copper-ore in bulk at the time of our visit. The Company appear to be doing well, judging by the number of steamers which call here for cargoes. The mine is 400 feet deep, and the shaft perpendicular. About 800 men are employed at the works, and the settlement is half a mile from the works, picturesquely situated at the head of the bay. Escorted by Mr Guzman, the manager, we descended the mine, and watched the operation of drilling and blasting the glittering metal. This is hoisted up to the mouth of the pit in the usual way, and from thence delivered by a tram-railroad direct into the vessel's hold. This mine is well ventilated, and as no accumulation of gas ever takes place, the lives of the miners are as free from danger as possible. They earn from 5s. to 6s. a-day (nominal), overseers 9s.; but as the men are obliged to get their provisions, clothing, &c., from the store attached to the establishment, very little cash ever reaches their pockets, I suspect. The fire at Hall's Bay approached very near to Little Bay, and at one time the magazine was seriously threatened. The miners dug trenches at the back of their huts—who but a miner would think of such a thing?—to bury their effects should the fire come upon them.

Having settled some disputes between Mr Guzman and his people, some of whom had established themselves on land belonging to the Company,[1] we proceeded to another mining port, called by the miners Robert's Arm, but not marked on our charts. A small copper-mine is being worked near Robert's Arm, and considerable money has been expended on it, the

---

[1] One man had built his house *below* high-water mark, and thus defied Mr Guzman to touch him. Of course the sea came round about the house every tide; but being built on piles, it did no harm. The case was referred to me for adjudication, and I gave it in favour of the man for his ingenuity. I doubt if the law could touch him in any case.

tramway alone being two miles long. It does not, however, pay its expenses, and instead of being a feeder to the mine at Little Bay, is a drain upon it; so it will soon in all probability be closed.[1]

The harbour is one of the most beautiful ones on the coast; and although the approach is somewhat intricate, it is sufficiently large to accommodate half-a-dozen large ships if moored. It is perfectly landlocked and steep-to, with deep water and good holding-ground. No man-of-war had ever entered it until H.M.S. Contest's visit last year; so the surprise and pleasure of the inhabitants may be well imagined at seeing the Druid and the Fantôme lying peacefully at anchor within pistol-shot of the rocks.

Another copper-mine is being worked in the south-west arm of Green Bay, and fresh discoveries are being constantly made in the neighbourhood. There is not the least doubt that all the coast, from Hall's Bay northward, is rich in minerals. Already most of it has been taken up by speculators, who look for-

[1] It has since been so.

ward to the good time coming, when the French shore question is settled, to work their claims.

From this snug anchorage we proceeded along the coast to the northward, touching at various places, settling many disputes, and laying down the law to those who pretended not to know it, till we found ourselves again in St Anthony Harbour (July 3d). The harbour was so crowded with schooners, we had great difficulty in threading our way amongst them. These vessels were all waiting for a slant of wind to sail for the coast of Labrador. Measles and diphtheria are making sad havoc amongst these poor folk at a small settlement called Goose Cove, six miles from St Anthony: seventeen people have died in the last three weeks from these causes. *There is no doctor on any part of this coast, and the people die like dogs,* for it is impossible for our surgeon to deal with an epidemic of this sort during our flying visits from place to place. The French doctors do what they can, but they have enough to do to look after their own people. Every French vessel carries a doctor, who attends to their own folk, and, to a great extent, to the English also, using their own medicines and making no charge for them. All honour to them for their humanity! A resident doctor should certainly be sent to this forsaken part of the coast. The poor people come any distance to see our doctors, but we cannot remain long enough to be of much permanent good.

July 4th.—Left St Anthony Harbour with *eleven* schooners in tow; several parted their hawsers outside as the breeze freshened, and made sail, dipping their colours, cheering, and firing their seal-guns in acknowledgment of our assistance. Arrived at Pistolet Bay the same afternoon. No inhabitants could be seen here; but the people belonging to Ha Ha Bay, a short distance across the isthmus, come over to bar the salmon-rivers, three of which discharge into the bay, as we saw where their weirs had been built. This neighbourhood is about the worst on the coast for quarrels between the French and English fishermen, and should be constantly visited.

Immense quantities of eider-duck breed in Pistolet Bay, the only place I ever saw them in Newfoundland. Thousands of these useful birds nest on the numerous islets scattered about the bay undisturbed either by man or vermin. Here a new industry awaits the settler: the eggs and down of these birds might be regularly collected as in Norway, and the result could not fail to be a profitable undertaking. It could hardly be maintained that this industry "interfered with the French in their fishing operations."

From this place we went round to Bonne Bay on the west coast, and found the usual quarrelling about land going on. The fact is, as there is no magistrate on any part of this coast since Captain Howarth's death, the law is set at defiance, and there is no one but a solitary policeman to enforce it.[1] The French are entirely answerable for this state of things, for they have always protested against the appointment of magistrates on this coast, and we have been weak enough to accede to it.

Hearing by telegraph that the French commodore was at Port Saunders in the Clorinde, I left for that place on the 8th, arriving there the same day.

[1] This evil has, I hope, now been removed.

Port Saunders is a first-rate anchorage, and conveniently near to Port au Choix, where the French have a large establishment and several ships. We were glad to find that in consequence of our action last year the two fine salmon-rivers at the head of Hawke's Bay were alive with salmon, several of which were transferred to the Druid.

The two culprits who have barred the rivers for so many years fled into the woods at the sight of the ship, leaving their nets upon the strand.

In consequence of a telegram from the Governor, I proceeded to St George's Bay on 13th July, to settle a matter there which caused a good deal of excitement at the time both at home and abroad. Some of the inhabitants at this place had lately refused to pay duties on a cargo of goods imported from Nova Scotia, alleging as an excuse that they were not represented in the local Parliament, and therefore ought not to be taxed. Moreover, they claimed that in so doing they had been supported by the French commodore. This proved not to be the case, although there appeared at the time to be some foundation for the statement. Be that as it may, the affair naturally gave rise to a good deal of tall-talk in the local and also in the English papers, and resulted in the question of representation and the appointment of magistrates being at last considered.[1] If these results are obtained, the fracas at St George's Bay will have done much good.

From St George we went to Cod Roy, a place seldom visited by a large ship, as the anchorage is by no means a safe one. There are about 400 inhabitants at Cod Roy proper; no doctor, clergyman, or magistrate. The people are a lawless lot, as might be supposed. The French have almost deserted the place, two Frenchmen only residing on Cod Roy Island, where they fish, and grow vegetables.

The valley of the Cod Roy river is one of the most fertile and thriving portions of the island. The pasturage is excellent, and the cattle and sheep raised here are second to none in any part of the world.

There is a scattered settlement on both banks of the river, mostly Roman Catholics. The

[1] I believe they have since been appointed.

Rev. Father Sears has resided amongst these people for thirteen years, and is most deservedly loved and respected. The river has a bar across it, and must be entered by a narrow channel, having nine feet water in it, a little to the south of the mouth proper. It is a broad and swift stream, but shallow, with numerous sand-bars in it. It is navigable for small craft for three or four miles, beyond which only flat-bottomed punts can ascend. The Cod Roy was once famous for salmon; but many years of wholesale netting have nearly exhausted it, and the yield is now barely sufficient for the people residing on the banks. The main channel is narrow, and is so thoroughly barred by stake and trap nets ingeniously set, that few fish can pass to the spawning-beds above. Being anxious to explore the river, I ascended it for twelve miles, accompanied by some of the officers, but not a fish could we see. Fortunately we had removed some of the nets on our way up; and the same night, whilst camped on the banks of the river, we heard the fish jumping in the pools. The next morning I hooked five grilse, and killed four of them before breakfast.

From Cod Roy we once more rounded Cape Ray, the western limit of the French fishing-ground, and cast anchor in the snug harbour of Port au Basque.

Not far from the anchorage, across a narrow neck of land, is a beautiful salmon-river called Grand Bay Brook, famous for salmon and trout of enormous size. I followed the stream from its source to the sea. There are three most picturesque falls about two or three miles apart, the finest being the one farthest from the sea. The river winds through a fine grass country, and a few settlers go there in the summer to cut hay. The best land and the best fishing are between the second and third falls from the mouth. Whilst at this place we received orders to meet the United States steamer Vandalia at Long Harbour, Fortune Bay, on the 25th July; so having first filled up with coal at Sydney, Cape Breton Island, we anchored once more in our old berth at the head of Long Harbour on the day appointed. We had thus made the complete circuit of the island—having called at every port worth going to, many on the south coast twice over—in exactly three months.

After a pleasant meeting with our American cousins, during which we discussed imaginary "outrages" over our cigars and champagne, we parted—the Vandalia for the States, whilst we continued our cruise. The same afternoon an accident befell the Druid which very nearly brought our cruising to a sudden and unexpected conclusion, and necessitated our going to Halifax for repairs. A few days at that charming spot soon put us to rights again, and by the 20th August we were again on our station endeavouring to grope our way into Channel Harbour in one of the thickest fogs I ever remember. Although close off the harbour-mouth—so close that we could hear the breakers all round us— we could see nothing. Our boats, looking for the entrance, were as helpless as ourselves. In this forlorn position a man fell overboard, and the engines, which had been at rest for some time previously, could not be moved. However, by firing guns we attracted some fishermen, who came off to pilot us in; and having recovered the man, we managed to creep in. This fog had lasted, with but slight intermission, for five weeks, enveloping sea and sky in one damp raw mist. The fishermen had been unable to dry their fish owing to the absence of sun, and had lost almost all their catch for the season.

These fogs are terribly depressing, besides being most dangerous. They come on without any warning, obscuring everything fifty yards beyond the ship. The best navigator is then helpless, and the only thing to be done is to grope along, taking every possible precaution, and trust to Providence. In this way we groped our way right into Harbour Briton one day, firing guns, sounding fog-horns, blowing steam-whistles, &c., the hoarse roar of the latter being bellowed back from the cliffs, and affording our only guide. Our boats were all away, but got lost themselves. At last we agreed we could go no farther. We could hear dogs barking, cocks crowing, but could see nothing. Presently a boat came to us out of the gloom. "Where is Harbour Briton?" we hailed. "You're *in* Harbour Briton," was the satisfactory answer, and a few yards farther on our anchor was dropped; but the boats did not find their way in for some hours afterwards. After cruising along the south coast for another fortnight, we returned to St John's on September 6th.

Having received a long string of protests and complaints from my French colleague, who had in the meanwhile sailed for France, we again started on the 26th September for the north-east coast to inquire into the same. The weather had now changed for the worse. Constant gales, accompanied by blinding squalls, delayed us somewhat, and we gladly took refuge once more in our old quarters in Robert's Arm; and it was not till the 15th October that we reached Kirpon, the northernmost point of the island, where most of the "outrages" were said to have occurred. Having investigated these matters, we returned to St John's, and took our final departure from the hospitable shores of Newfoundland a few days afterwards.

CHAPTER VI.

THE ABORIGINES OF NEWFOUNDLAND—THE MICMACS—TRAPPING—GENERAL DESCRIPTION OF GAME BIRDS—ANIMALS AND FISH, ETC.

I BEG to inform the reader that the next few chapters will be devoted to sport with the gun, rod, or rifle. They form a series of letters written to the 'Field' under the *nom de plume* of "Mariner"; and they were subsequently printed in pamphlet form in St John's. This little work ran through two editions, and is now sold out; but the letters, written freshly at the time, recall vividly to my mind the various scenes I have attempted to describe. I therefore make no apology for reproducing them now, with a few alterations, which subsequent experience makes desirable.

Of the original inhabitants of Newfoundland no trace remains, except a few stone arrow-heads, which are occasionally discovered on the shores of Grand Pond and Red Indian Lake. All that is known of them is, that they were a hardy race, living by hunting and trapping, as do their successors, the Micmac Indians, at the present day.

In the year 1822, Lieutenant Buchan, of H.M.S. Grasshopper, went up the Exploits river in order to discover some of the Red Indians, with a view to their civilisation; but with no results. A Red Indian woman was captured near one of the brooks running into Nôtre Dame Bay, and her husband was said to have been shot at the time: she was brought to St John's, but died of consumption. Another woman, named Shawnadithit, was captured on the Exploits river, and was also brought to St John's, where she lived for several years. It is certain that there are none of the tribe left; in all probability the last of them was killed by the Micmacs. Of these latter, there are probably not more than 100 in the whole island, who are distributed about the coast, mostly at Hall's Bay and the Bay of Despair, and even these are fast dying out. These Indians, who emigrated originally from Nova Scotia, live entirely by hunting and trapping, by which they earn a good deal of money, and are in all respects more independent than the white trappers, whom they hold in supreme contempt. They are far better hunters and trappers, and are not to be excelled at lumbering, boat-building, poling up rivers, and all the incidents of a backwoodsman's craft. They know every inch of the country, and will follow a trail with the sagacity of an animal; and, as a rule, are fairly sober and honest, although they have the credit of being exactly the reverse. The Indian leaves his home in early spring, and takes to the woods in quest of beavers, otters, foxes, and marten-cats. Beaver-skins pay best, as they are most plentiful, a good trapper being able to kill as many as thirty to forty in a week, and probably average two a-day through the season. The following is the average value of skins, taking one year with another; but the price of fur fluctuates so much that these quotations must be considered only approximate :—

	£	s.	d.
Black fox (very rare)	15	0	0
Silver fox	8	0	0
Grey or patch fox	1	10	0
Common red fox	0	8	0
Otter (according to quality)	1	10	0
Beaver (by weight)	0	16	0
Black bear (according to size)	2	0	0
White bear (do. do.)	5	0	0
Caribou (not much used)	0	15	0
Wolf (Government price)	2	10	0
Marten-cat (a kind of sable)	0	15	0

The Government offers a reward of twelve dollars for each wolf-skin; but it is not often claimed, owing to the extraordinary sagacity of the animal, which makes it difficult to shoot, trap, or poison him. I believe also that wolves are scarce. I have seen their tracks, but I have never come across one of them.

Having obtained all the skins he can pack on his back or stow in his canoe, the Indian, as the winter draws near, establishes himself on the banks of a lake where the deer are in the habit of crossing in their annual migrations from north to south; he then kills what he wants for his winter's supply of meat, and makes tracks for home, where he disposes of his furs to the traders in exchange for pork, flour, tea, molasses, tobacco, and suchlike necessaries of life. The Indians are often accused of slaughtering deer and beaver in a wholesale way, but of this I feel confident they are guiltless. These animals supply them with food, and they could not exist without them, therefore it is their interest to protect them, and they only kill what they require. Not so the white settlers, who openly boast of the number of deer they slaughter, for the sake of their horns and skin, in the winter time when the poor animals are half starved. I am sorry to say that parties of Englishmen, calling themselves sportsmen, have also been guilty of this butchery, one party having, some years ago, massacred over one hundred, leaving their carcasses to rot upon the ground.

The only deer in the island is the caribou, or wood reindeer—a noble animal, inferior in size only to the moose and wapiti. These animals roam over the barrens or highlands by thousands; they may be killed in the manner above mentioned, or stalked in true Highland fashion,—the latter method being the only one worthy of a real sportsman.

Foremost among game birds is the grouse, or, as it is called in the country, partridge, and is identical with the Norwegian *ryper*. Its proper name is *Lagopus albus*, or willow-grouse. The ptarmigan *Lagopus rupestris*, called in Newfoundland the rock-partridge, is also found in some parts of the island, but is more rare, and is similar in appearance and habits to the Scotch ptarmigan. Grouse are numerous all over the island; the coveys average from eight to twelve, and afford good sport, except in the interior, where they are so tame they may be knocked down with a stick. The best bird for the table is the Esquimaux curlew (*Numenius borealis*), which makes its appearance on the shores of Labrador and the northern part of Newfoundland in August, preparatory to its annual migration to warmer latitudes. Unlike the larger species common in the British Isles, these birds are delicious eating, whether cooked fresh or potted. They arrive in immense flocks, feeding greedily upon the blue-berries, which are plentiful on the barrens, coming down to the sea-shore at low water, and returning as the tide rises. So plump are they that they sometimes burst on falling to the ground; and so stupid, that, after firing both barrels into a flock, the remainder invariably wheel round to see what is the matter. In this way many hundreds are killed, and if not a very sportsmanlike proceeding, it is certainly excusable, as the birds are highly esteemed. By September they have all left the country, probably for the swampy marshes about New Orleans, from whence, I suspect, but few return.

CHAPTER VII.

THE FAUNA OF NEWFOUNDLAND.

WILD geese are numerous in all parts of the island—breeding in the ponds of the interior, and also in the neighbourhood of Cape Race. There are, I believe, two kinds; but the only one I have ever seen is the Canada goose (*Bernicla canadensis*), a very handsome bird with a black neck. They are easily domesticated, and cross readily with the ordinary farmyard goose, the result being the mongrel goose so much esteemed by epicures. Wild-goose shooting in Newfoundland is really splendid sport, and requires more careful stalking than deer-stalking, the birds being excessively wary, and always having a sentry posted, like the rest of their kind. The best chance is on the wing, when the Indians, and many white men also, can call them down within shot. The plan adopted is to imitate the "cry" of the bird, and, keeping out of sight, to wave a white handkerchief to and fro; the geese, if within hearing, invariably fly down to the ruse, probably taking the handkerchief for one of their species flapping its wings. A curious thing also is that a dog will attract them, especially if it be a red one: they take it for a fox, and, instead of flying away, come towards it. I have seen this several times. One man told me he had seen a fox calling the geese to him by imitating their cry. There is no doubt the fox is cunning enough to do it, and I believe they are fools enough to respond. Of wild ducks there are several kinds. The commonest and the best for the table is the black duck, a very wary bird. Eider-ducks are plentiful in Pistolet Bay, the only place I ever saw them; and mergansers, called by the natives "shell birds," are also very common.

Loons (the great northern diver) may be seen and heard upon any of the lakes of the interior. Snipe are tolerably plentiful in the Peninsula of Avalon, but very rare elsewhere. Sandpipers of many kinds abound, also several kinds of plover; but woodcocks are unknown, which is the more remarkable, seeing the splendid coverts for them. I believe they might be imported from Nova Scotia or Cape Breton. Black-game ought also to do well, as they thrive in Norway, an almost similar country.

There is only one kind of bear in the island, the common black species. They are numerous in the south coast, especially in the neighbourhood of Hare Bay, the Bay of Despair, White Bear Bay, &c.—in fact, those parts which are uninhabited, or very sparsely so—also about Hawke's Bay, on the west coast, and on the coast of Labrador. Polar bears are sometimes met with on the ice in the Straits of Belleisle, but very rarely on the coast. An old settler told me of an adventure he had with one of these animals. He saw a white bear asleep on the ice, so he went after him with his heavy seal-gun, and accompanied by a little dog. When they got close to, the dog began barking, and woke the bear, who, taking in the situation, went for the man. The seal-gun missed fire, as they often do; the man turned to run, but the bear overtook him and knocked him down. Falling on his back, he had the presence of mind to feign death, and held in his breath. The bear smelt his face, and then, supposing him to be dead, walked off; and the man did so likewise, in the opposite direction, as soon as possible.

Wolves are said to be common; but I do not believe they are so numerous as people suppose. My reason for saying so is, that I have never known the carcass of a deer disturbed, although it has remained on the ground for several days. I do not think they do so much harm as they are credited with, and certainly not so much as the packs of half-wild, half-starved curs which infest the country in the neighbourhood of the settlements. If Government were to give a reward for every one of these brutes that was shot, only allowing a certain number to the settlers, it would be more to the purpose. They are, without doubt, the curse of the country, no farmer being able to keep sheep or cattle for fear of them. These brutes are not fed, except occasionally on seal-blubber, when it can be got, and are left to get their own living. They are supposed to have a huge log tied round their necks, to prevent them hunting sheep; but this law is not enforced except in the towns.

The settlers keep them for hauling lumber out of the woods in the winter time, and no doubt they are useful in that way; but they should be kept in proper order, their numbers limited, and their owners made responsible for them. Horses will of course do this work far better, as I have seen at Hall's Bay, but a horse is a more expensive animal to keep. I don't suppose many of the poor settlers have ever seen a horse. One was landed some years ago on Merasheen Island in Placentia Bay: it was a white beast, and the settlers thought it was a caribou, and shot it. The caribou turn white in winter—as do the hares. These latter are the same as the blue Scotch hares, which they resemble, but are larger, and are tolerably numerous all over the island. The American hare (*Lepus americanus*), commonly called rabbit, was only introduced a few years ago. They have now spread all over the island, and must form a very acceptable change of diet to the settler and his poor half-starved, badly clothed family.

On our visits round the island, we met with sights enough to sicken us, and make us ashamed to think that these poor creatures were British subjects like ourselves. On many parts of Labrador, the west coast of Newfoundland, and on parts of the north-east coast, the people are starving every winter, though it is the custom in St John's to laugh at these reports as gross exaggerations. I can only say that we have seen this state of things repeatedly: any one who has followed our cruise round the coast cannot fail to have remarked it; but as long as everything is sacrificed to the fishing, and these dogs permitted, there is no help for it. But for these brutal dogs, sheep-farming might be encouraged, and the women taught to spin and weave the wool, to make clothes for themselves and their little ones, as they do in the Highlands of Scotland, instead of going about in that climate scantily clothed, and their wretched children half naked, because they are too poor to buy any clothes, or the material to make them. These poor creatures used to flock on board to see the doctor at every port, asking for medicines, when it was patent to all that what they wanted was nourishing food and warm clothing, in lieu of molasses and fish to eat, with barely sufficient clothes for decency, and those of the most paltry material. I may be accused of exaggeration in these details, and naturally so; for there is hardly any one living in the island who could or would admit the facts, because they cannot have come under their observation. If any magistrate or doctor, where there is one round the coast, was asked if it was the case, he would probably say no; because it is not so at the principal places where magistrates and doctors are to be found. But ask the clergymen, who go to the outposts, their opinion; ask Mr Curling — a gentleman who shoulders his knapsack, and tramps through the snow for days together, sharing his frugal meal with the poor creatures he visits, — he could describe in far more graphic terms than I can pretend to, the state of these unfortunates. But naval officers have far better opportunities than any one else of observation, seeing that they are constantly visiting places that many

Newfoundlanders have never heard of, and certainly never seen. And yet I believe I am within the mark in saying that no less than 100,000 dollars is paid annually in pauper relief, out of a total population of 180,000!

Possibly some of the many rich and charitable persons who are in the habit of sending out money or clothing to black savages, who don't require it, might, out of their superfluity, contribute a trifle to these poor folk. The officers of her Majesty's ships would gladly distribute any gift, free of expense; blankets and flannel would be most acceptable; the few blankets we were able to spare from our private stores were always gratefully appreciated. If the settlers could keep goats, it would be a help to them, a goat being the poor man's cow,—a hardy beast, that gets his own living. But, before all, death to the dogs! I have, however, been led away by this subject, and must return to sport.

Next, with regard to fishing.

To say that rod-fishing in Newfoundland is a delusion and a snare would perhaps be wide of the mark, and yet I have no hesitation in saying that any one going out to that country for the purpose of fishing only, would be disappointed: as regards salmon he most certainly would. Sea-trout fishing is merely a question of being on the right spot at the right time, in which case the sport is second to none; but if the fish are not running, the sport is *nil*.

I speak from three years' experience on the coast, during which I have had unusual facilities for prosecuting this fascinating sport, having wetted a line in almost every likely-looking river round the island, and a few in Labrador. The first year's experience proved that it was of no use fishing for sea-trout much before the 20th July (except perhaps at Biscay Bay, near Trepassey, an early river), about which time these fish arrive on the coast and begin to ascend the rivers. From that time the sport steadily improves, and some fine baskets can be made. Our second and third cruise told precisely the same tale; although in one case we went round by the south and west coasts, descending by the north—on the other two, *vice versâ*.

Salmon-fishing with the fly may be pronounced a failure owing to two causes,—one of which may be remedied, the other not. The first is, because the whole of the fine salmon-rivers are ruined by barring, sweeping with nets, traps, weirs, or mill-dams, in defiance of all laws and proclamations, till the wretched fish are almost exterminated, all the large breeding-fish being captured, and only a few grilse escaping. The other reason is, that the fish do not as a rule rise to the fly. I have occasionally taken grilse with the fly, but only five the first season, eight the second, and about the same number the third. However, this represented many days' hard work, wading for ten and twelve hours a-day, and fishing every likely pool. In some of these places, where the rivers had not been barred, the fish would be disporting themselves all over the pool, but would not look at a fly. I conclude the Newfoundland salmon have not as yet been educated to the fly, though sometimes an occasional youngster does rise and get hooked; but these are the exceptions to the rule. I believe, however, that if you have the luck to be on the water just as a fresh run of salmon enter the river, or if you can spare the time to camp by the river and bide your time, good sport may be had with fly.

In corroboration of these remarks, I may state that a friend of mine has since enjoyed wonderful sport on one of the Newfoundland rivers. I claim to have indirectly assisted in his success, for this river was barred and netted in a shameful manner when I visited it; and although I killed some grilse above the nets, we saw no large salmon. We removed the obstacles, and would have confiscated them, but for the intercession of the priest in charge of the settlement. In consideration of his reverence's assurance that he would excommunicate any subsequent offender, I returned the nets to the owners. In this case the result has exceeded my most sanguine expectations.

With regard to the question of barring the rivers, this evil might be easily remedied. A few "guardians" stationed round the coast, paid by the Government as in Canada, would soon make a clean sweep of the nets, or at all events oblige them to be set in a legitimate manner, with a close-time as in Scotland. If this measure were adopted, so prolific is the *Salmo salar*, that the rivers would soon be so far improved as to be eagerly sought after by sportsmen from the old country, who would gladly pay the "guardians" themselves. At present, with a few notable exceptions, they are scarcely worth wetting a line in.

The process of barring a river is to stretch a net across from bank to bank, staked up above high-water mark. This is backed up by another net, placed directly behind it, which is of smaller mesh than the first, so that if a fish can manage to pass the first net, he is sure to be caught in the second. In this way I once counted seven nets, one behind the other. Of course all this is illegal, the law permitting a net to be set from the bank extending to one-third across the water, but this would never suit the Newfoundlander. Even if his net does not reach the opposite bank, he takes care to bar the deep-water channel, up which fish always go; and not content with that, he sets his net with a "trap" at the end, or middle, as the case may be, so that nothing can escape. I will endeavour to show my meaning by two

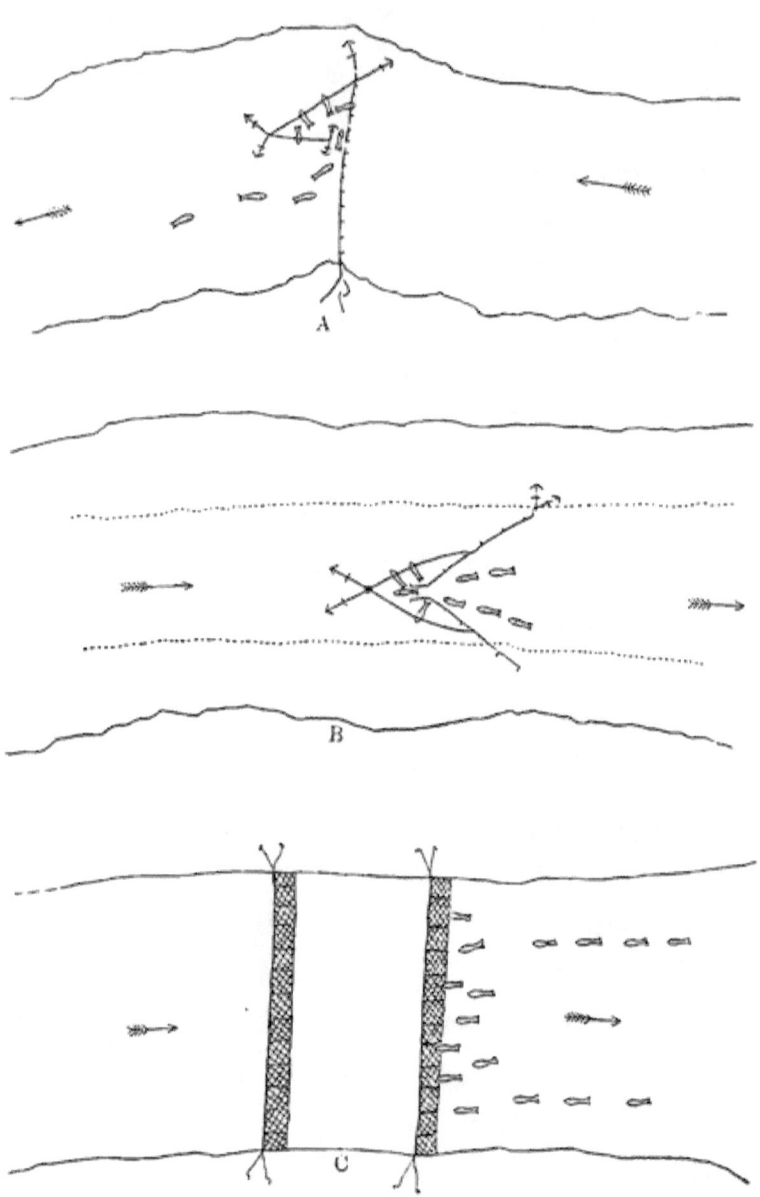

sketches, showing the trap at the end and also in the middle of the net.

The plans A, B, and C will show three of the methods of barring a river, as practised in Newfoundland; they speak for themselves, and require but little description.

In the first, A, it is evident that any fish coming up-stream and meeting the net, turn aside, endeavour to get round it, and go straight into the trap, from which they never escape. Finding themselves surrounded by nets, they make a dash for it and get meshed: nine fish out of every ten are found in the "trap." This net is illegally set, because it stretches two-thirds across the river instead of one-third; the mesh also being invariably too small.

In B a net is set in the form of a V, with a trap at the apex. The fish dash through this, and are caught in the net beyond it: they never attempt to go back through the trap, as they naturally force their way up-stream. This net is illegally set, since it bars the deep-water channel, up which the fish must pass; and its form is also illegal.

C requires no description. It completely bars the river, and the mesh is also too small. Nothing can possibly pass this net, or, if it did, the second would stop it. Illegal is no name for this method.

It must not be supposed that we, skippers and J.P.'s as we were, looked on calmly while these atrocities were being perpetrated, except in the case of the Frenchmen, when, alas! we were powerless. "By virtue of the authority invested in us," we were justified in proceeding against the offenders; but what was the use? One cannot get blood out of a stone, so the most we could do was to take up the nets, when so placed; but it was not always easy to do so, because they were generally taken up as soon as a man-of-war hove in sight, only to be replaced as soon as she was round the corner. It has been our good fortune, however, on one or two occasions to catch some of these individuals before they have unbuttoned their eyelids in the morning: the result has been most satisfactory.

One instance will suffice to show that I have not exaggerated the mischief done on the one hand, nor the good results accruing from the suppression of the same.

Having reason to suspect that a lovely salmon-river in Bonne Bay was barred, and had been so for twenty years, I left the ship at midnight in the steam cutter, towing a boat of light draught. We had twelve miles to go to the mouth of the river, which we reached just as dawn was breaking. The first object we saw was a boat with one man in it, making up the river as fast as possible; but, alas for him! not fast enough.

We were soon alongside, when, with a cheery "Good morning," we asked if there was any prospect of sport up the river.

"No, sir; not a great deal."

"Then you don't think it worth while putting up the rod even for a cast?"

"No, sir; I hardly think it is. There hasn't been a fish in this river for many years."

"Well, it *is* a pity, after coming so far, to be disappointed. I think I'll just wet a line."

The old sinner's face dropped, and he disappeared into the bush, while we proceeded. We had not gone a mile further before a sight met us enough to make any true angler collapse. Right across the river, from bank to bank, staked high above the water, was a splendid net, and suspended in the meshes, just as the water had left them, were several salmon and some noble trout, of 3 and 4 lb. weight. Above this net were three others, all containing fish; and above that again—not a living thing, and no wonder. Chucking away our rods, gaffs, &c., we set to work, lifted all the nets, and put them in the boat, together with the fish; drew the stakes, and sent them down the stream; and then dropped down the river to enjoy our breakfast, which we felt we had earned. Presently our old friend hove in sight.

"Well, sir, did you have any sport?"

"Yes, thank you, pretty fair, and better than I expected,"—at the same time holding up a fine salmon.

"Lor', sir, you don't say so! I really didn't expect," &c., &c.

"Yes; and the next time I come I hope to have better; for if ever I catch you again, you will be fined fifty dollars in addition to the confiscation of your nets."

The old reprobate didn't wait to hear more, but retired into the bush with the "compliments of the season."

At the same time that this was taking place, another of our boats, in charge of the first lieutenant (also J.P.), went down the coast to the mouth of a celebrated trout-stream. Arriving on the scene at daylight, he found eight nets set across the river, one above another. Sweeping away the whole of these, to the irrepressible disgust of the natives, our boat returned on board, our united bag for the morning's work being twelve nets and a fine haul of fish.

As a sequel to this story, I must mention that the following year I again visited this salmon-river in company with a youngster eleven years of age. We poled up the river as far as we could, waded a mile or so more, and then found ourselves at a likely-looking pool, below which was a rapid, or "rattle," as it is called in that country.

Selecting one of Farlow's lovely "silver doctors," I commenced at the head of the pool, whilst Jim fished below. About one-third down, a rise, and I was fast in a 3-lb. trout, which was speedily landed; and to cut the story short, I took eighteen others between 2 and 3 lb. each out of that pool before I left it. I then moved down to help Jim, who could not reach the further bank, where the fish were lying. At this place we found the trout jostling each other. So thick were they, that although there were salmon in the pool—for we could see them—the latter stood no chance, as the more nimble trout seized the fly immediately it touched the water. For upwards of an hour the fun was fast and furious, and we were constantly both playing fish at the same time. The bank was sloping and clear of trees, so we gave them the butt freely, and after a few rushes, hauled them out by the hair of the head! The strand looked as if a seine had been hauled, speckled beauties of 3 and 4 lb. lying about in all directions. At last the fish slacked off, as well they might, and we hove to for a cup of coffee, which was prepared for us on the bank. After a short spell for refreshment, and to rest the water, we set to work again; but the trout had had enough of our flies. I rose a salmon at the tail of the pool, and Jim hooked another, which he lost. We then fished the pool over again, with a small trout on spinning-tackle, taking three brace more big trout, after which I went up to the first pool and killed a grilse with the fly, and half-a-dozen more trout.

It was now 3 P.M., and we had a long journey before us, so, putting our fish into the skiff, which had been poled up whilst we were fishing, we dropped down the river and then went on board. Our bag weighed exactly 98 lb., out of which there were thirteen trout which scaled over 3 lb. and twenty-five over 2 lb. —not a bad bag to be made between 11 A.M. and 3 P.M. I think I am justified therefore in saying, that, given fair play, the rivers of Newfoundland would be second to none in any part of the world.

The above represents an exceptionally good day's sport, even for Newfoundland—certainly the best I ever had. As a rule, I should consider from 20 to 30 lb. weight a good basket for that country; and several times I have brought that weight back after a hard day's work.

CHAPTER VIII.

A DAY AMONGST THE GRILSE.

In our chart of Hall's Bay I had often noticed a fall of 127 feet marked on a celebrated salmon-river called the Indian Brook, only three miles from its mouth. Being desirous of seeing the wonderful fall, I engaged two Indians to pole me up the river in a canoe; so we started one lovely morning in July, a little before daybreak. There is a steam saw-mill at the mouth of the brook, and great quantities of lumber are rafted down the stream to be cut up at this mill. Trailing my salmon-fly astern of the canoe, I hooked and killed a lively grilse. The roar of the falls could now be distinctly heard, and soon afterwards a bend in the river brought us in sight of them; but I must say I was sadly disappointed. Instead of 127 feet, I estimate the falls at not over 20, if so much: they must have shrunk since they were surveyed.[1] A mass of logs, many of large size, had formed a jam at the falls, completely blocking the passage, and raising the water several feet, thus preventing any fish from ascending. The foaming torrent poured over and through these logs with a deafening roar. Close below the fall was a deep still pool, in which the water glided silently to some rapids below; at the lower part of this pool was another jam of logs, — the heavy spars were thrown about in every possible position like spillicans. Stepping out upon the rocks overhanging the silent pool, I dropped my fly lightly upon the water. Instantly there was a gleam like silver out of the depths, the line tautened, — a fresh-run grilse sprang out of the water, was all over the pool, — and in three minutes he was cleverly netted by one of the Indians, and lay gasping on the bank.

[1] I have since heard from Mr Murray, who surveyed this part of the country, that the height ought to have been 12.7 feet, which he judged it to be.

After a short spell to rest the pool and enjoy a cup of coffee and a cigar, I took up my rod again, and hooked another grilse with the third cast, which, after several leaps, went over the fall below, and was landed lower down. A few more throws, and I was fast in another; this one also went over the falls, but left my fly sticking in a log; and the next one served me the same way. A fifth landed on the logs in his first jump, and we parted company. After this I had no more luck, although I rose and hooked several more: they all went over the falls or hung me up in the logs, in spite of all I could do to prevent them. Had it not been for these logs, I must have had at least a dozen of them, for they took the fly well and were all fair hooked. After this the salmon left off rising, and I took six heavy trout, averaging 3 lb. each, and returned to the ship, not over-satisfied with my day's work. Two days afterwards I returned to the spot, taking Jim with me, and had the pleasure of seeing the little fellow kill his first salmon. We got three that day, and as many big trout, by 7 A.M., when it came on to rain, and the fish ceased to rise. This river had not been netted, and was full of fish, and I have no doubt first-rate sport might have been had there, but our short stay prevented any further enjoyment of it.

One of the objections to fishing in Newfoundland is the difficulty of getting to the best places, as the coastal steamers do not necessarily call at them. A small coaster might be easily hired by a party of sportsmen, and probably good sport enjoyed; but everything in the shape of provisions, &c., including a tent, must be taken, as no sort of accommodation can be found on any part of the coast.

The mosquitoes and black flies are a very great nuisance during the summer months; but the same applies to all the rivers in Canada, Nova Scotia, Norway, &c., and although undoubtedly a great drawback, they are not sufficient to deter a keen angler from enjoying his favourite pastime. We found the best remedy to be Stockholm tar and oil, or carbolic and oil— twenty parts of the latter to one of the former —the flies buzz round, but they don't hanker after it. As to veils, I wouldn't be bothered with them. They are all very well for loch-fishing, or where you have no distance to walk; but when, as in Newfoundland, you have often to walk for miles to reach the water, or wade up the river to reach the pools—climbing over boulders, with an occasional header into the river—a veil would be worse than useless; besides, it is uncomfortably hot, interferes with smoking, and you cannot see your fly, or a fish rise.

As regards dress, ordinary Scotch tweeds are the best, with thick stockings, and nailed boots. Wading is indispensable; but in summer the water is not too cold, and after a rub down and a change, one is none the worse for it. If a man must wear waders, he had better stick to Scotland, where he has to stand in a pool all day; but they will not do where you have often to walk half-a-dozen miles to the water, and back again over a very rough country; besides, as there are no roads, one has generally to take the bed of the stream for it.

The unsophisticated natives, mostly Irishmen, have no sort of idea of distance. If one of them tells you the river is five miles off, you may make up your mind to a good three hours' tramp, and are lucky if you find it then; so the best way, if you find a good pool, is to pitch your camp there, and stick to it.

Although sea-fishing hardly comes under the name of sport, a few words on the subject may be of interest.

The cod is the only fish recognised in Newfoundland as of any value, except perhaps the halibut. All others are looked upon merely as bait, or for manuring the ground. I have even known trout of 3 and 4 lb. weight cut up as bait for cod; and the man that told me this wasn't a bit ashamed of himself.

The Newfoundland cod has for many years commanded the markets of Spain, Brazil, and the West Indies; but of late the Norwegian and Iceland fisheries have been running them very closely, if they have not run them off the field, and monopolised the trade as regards Spain. This is said to be due to the superior manner in which the Norwegian fish is made or cured; and also that the Norwegians have been able to undersell the Newfoundlanders; there is no fear, however, but that the latter will always maintain a high place in market value. The bank fishery on the coasts of Newfoundland and Labrador is probably equal to that of all the rest of the world put together; and when it is estimated that a cod's roe contains from 4 to 9 million eggs, there is little fear of this fish being exterminated. The average size of cod is probably 7 or 8 lb.; but I have known of a single fish weighing as much as a quintal, or 112 lb.!

Herrings abound in such prodigious numbers that no just estimate could be formed of them. They are frequently barred in any of the numerous estuaries along the coast, such as Long Harbour, by enclosing them in long deep nets, and kept in this manner until vessels arrive to take them away. This method is illegal, and very properly so, as many millions die of starvation or suffocation, and sink to the bottom. I have heard of the bottom of the sea being covered with dead herrings to the depth of 16 feet. Even with our small service seine we have taken 60,000 herrings at a single haul, and been obliged to open out the seine and allow the bulk of them to escape, to prevent the net breaking.

These fish are nearly all used for manure, although they are fully as good as the Scotch herrings. Halibut are taken off Cape Ray, weighing as much as 500 lb. each; and mackerel are also tolerably numerous.

The caplin—a most delicious little fish, belonging to the family of *Salmonidæ*—arrive on the coast about June, in countless millions; and it is no exaggeration to say that the very colour of the sea is changed by their presence. They are followed by shoals of cod, salmon, and trout, which prey upon them; and so terrified are the poor little fish that they cast themselves ashore, and the whole coast is covered with their remains. They are used chiefly for bait and for manure; but they are also excellent eating, whether fresh or dried. In the latter state they are imported to Great Britain, though not in large quantities. In appearance the caplin somewhat resemble the smelt.

Squids, belonging to the family of cuttle-fish (*Cephalopoda*), are very numerous, and are used largely for bait. The fishermen catch them by jigging—*i.e.*, lowering down a lead weight armed with hooks, and jigging it up and down through the shoal. Some enormous specimens of the octopus have been caught on the coast, the arms of some of these creatures measuring 30 to 40 feet. These formidable monsters are much dreaded by the fishermen.

CHAPTER IX.

GROUSE-SHOOTING.

Any one who chooses to work hard and has a good dog may get very good grouse-shooting in any part of Newfoundland. The Peninsula of Avalon abounds with grouse, and even in the immediate neighbourhood of St John's there are plenty; but there are also plenty of gunners in that locality, so that it is necessary to go some little distance to make a bag. The neighbourhood of Trepassey is a famous beat, so is Cape Race, Cape Pine, St Mary's Peninsula. Wherever you may go, birds will be found in numbers to satisfy any sportsman who prefers to see dogs working, and walking up the birds, to squatting behind stone walls and having them driven over his head. But good dogs are absolutely necessary; even with one only, a fair bag may be got. I have worked most of the ground above-mentioned, besides many other places—such as Bay de Nord, Ship Cove in the Bay of Despair, Hare Bay, White Bear Bay, La Poile, all on the south coast—with one old setter, "Paddy," who has been my faithful companion for years; and had fair sport at every one of them. Many is the time we have tramped for hours without seeing a feather; but we almost always dropped on to them before the day was out, and managed to pick up eight or ten brace, which I call a good bag for a rough wild country, where every man carries a gun and shoots where he pleases. There is a regular close season, else the broods would soon be exterminated; and the 1st September is the opening day as in England, for these birds are called partridges out there, although they are nothing of the kind.

The grouse lie uncommonly close, and the cover is very thick, so they are not always easy to find, but, when found, are not difficult to shoot. I have frequently killed eight or nine out of a covey without moving—as they get up singly or in twos, as if out of a bag. The settlers always choose a foggy day, when the birds are loath to rise, and shoot them on the ground three or four at a shot; but they are not to be blamed for that, seeing that a charge from one of their seal-guns means half a handful of powder and " five fingers " of buckshot. In the interior the grouse are so tame they will not rise, and afford no sport; and I have often, when out after deer, seen the Indians knock them over with a stone or with an axe.

One of the most delightful expeditions I know of, combining sport with beautiful scenery, may be had by driving from St John's to Salmonier, a place we often visited in the Druid; but only once did I have the good fortune or the time to go by land.[1] The road is a good one, and the scenery grand and beautiful throughout. From the heights above " Topsail Heads " a magnificent view of Conception Bay, with its islands and bold headlands, can be obtained on a clear day; and from thence a road winds through lovely and varied scenes

[1] There is now a railroad to Topsail and Holyrood.

to Holyrood, at the head of Conception Bay, where comfortable quarters are to be found.

Holyrood is twenty-eight miles from St John's, a little more than half-way to Salmonier. After leaving this place the sea is left behind, and the scene changes: from thence to Salmonier the drive is through dense pine-woods, with occasional clearings or open "barrens," interspersed with lovely lakes nestling in the woods,—in fact a thoroughly sporting-looking country, such as may be seen in many parts of Scotland and in Norway. At the half-way house, the only break between Holyrood and Salmonier, a fine view of the general features of the country is obtained; but, as I am a poor hand at descriptions of scenery, I shall not attempt to delineate them. The hotel at Salmonier is small and unpretentious, and Mr Carew and his wife are most obliging to their guests. Fair sport may be had in this neighbourhood with gun, rod, or rifle, according to the season. A snipe-marsh lies directly in front of the house; a salmon-river, to use an advertising phrase, "runs through the property;" and at the back of the premises, a few hours' journey through the woods, there is an extensive "park," or open barrens, where deer and wild geese are to be found in the fall of the year.

Escorted by an amusing guide of Irish extraction, I once visited this place after wild geese, and although the limited time at my disposal prevented me from seeing any game, the expedition was most enjoyable. "Pat" had, it seems, piloted a noble sportsman to these hunting-grounds after caribou; and he related with much gusto how he had succeeded in bagging a fawn after firing fourteen shots at it, his companion also distinguishing himself by killing a pricket, which he decapitated with a regimental sword, bearing the proud trophy into camp, and leaving the carcass to rot upon the ground.

But these exploits scarcely represent the sport that may be enjoyed on these barrens, and I have no doubt that good stags may be sometimes killed there. Our guide on this occasion brought with him a huge weapon, with a barrel like the main-topgallant mast of a frigate. This formidable engine he charged with "five fingers" of powder and the same liberal allowance of buckshot, and on my venturing to suggest that perhaps the gun might be overcharged, he said "she" always took that! but that on one occasion when the powder was rather better than usual, "she" knocked him down senseless in the snow, the hammer scalping him as the weapon disappeared over his head. On coming to, he discovered the gun buried in the snow ten yards behind him, and a deer which he had fired at lying dead, as well it might be, with five-and-twenty buckshot in its carcass.

I made an expedition to Salmonier one September, accompanied by an enthusiastic sporting judge of St John's. It rained heavily the whole way, and we were thoroughly soaked when we got to the hotel. However, a night's rest put us all to rights; and the next morning we started before daylight and drove down by the river's bank till we came abreast of a small "fore-and-after," with whose skipper we had made arrangements to take us over to the other side of St Mary's Bay. The crew had not yet roused out, so we opened fire on the craft with snipe-shot at forty yards, and after peppering the side and masts with several rounds, a shaggy head appeared above the gunwale to know what was wanted. We soon got aboard, and in a short time were scudding down the river with a flowing sheet; a smart north-east breeze carried us across the bay to a small harbour thirty miles distant, where we landed, and conveyed our traps to a farmhouse. We received a hearty welcome from our host, and indeed from all the village: the natives crowded round us, to give us every information concerning sport. These people all spoke with a foreign accent, rolling their "r's" like a Frenchman, but with a curious mixture of Irish brogue as well. They declared the "patterridges" to be jostling each other on the barrens; and as for trout and salmon, they were as thick as "the sands on the say." The village was picturesquely situated in a valley, and presented a very pleasing and well-to-do appearance, quite in contrast to the generality of Newfoundland settlements; this was due to the fact that the valley afforded pasturage to herds of cattle and sheep, and a considerable part of it was devoted to agriculture. The houses were beautifully clean and well kept; and the bonnie faces of the lassies, and the rosy chubby cheeks of the children, were delightful and refreshing to behold, and in pleasing contrast with the misery and desolation usually visible at the other settlements round the coast. This village of "Branch River" represents what a Newfoundland settlement ought to be, and what they would be, if any care were bestowed upon them. A fine salmon-river winds through the valley, irrigating a considerable extent of land, and forcing its way by a narrow "barachois"[1] to the sea.

I never saw finer potatoes, or better cream, bread, butter, or fatter poultry or stock, in any place than at Branch River, showing what can be done by perseverance. The hay crops were magnificent, and the whole place bore the aspect of a well-to-do farm in the Lowlands of Scotland. It is certainly the most flourishing little place in Newfoundland. The harbour is not a safe one, except for small craft that can enter the river; hence Branch is but little known.

The afternoon of our arrival we ascended the

[1] A narrow gorge.

barrens, and bagged sixteen brace of grouse and a few snipe. The birds were fairly plentiful; the dogs worked well; and the powder was straight. We spent three most pleasant days with our hospitable entertainers, enjoying good sport and keen bracing weather. On the fourth day we worked along the coast to a rendezvous, whither our boat had preceded us, and from thence re-crossed to Salmonier. Our bag (two guns) was sixty brace of grouse and a few couple of snipe—not much to brag of in a country where game is preserved; but not bad for a wild country, where the only protection the birds get is a close-time during the breeding-season—where every man carries a gun, and vermin are encouraged for the sake of their skins.

Walking on the barrens of Newfoundland is very much harder work than on a Scotch moor; but there is no limit to the extent of ground—it costs nothing. The birds, when found, are magnificent; and when the sport is combined with snug quarters and kind-hearted hospitality, it is not to be despised.

CHAPTER X.

THE CARIBOU AND CARIBOU-STALKING.

This noble animal (*Cervus tarandus*) is distributed all over the northern parts of Europe and America; and is also abundant in Newfoundland and Labrador. In Lapland, Norway, and Iceland, it is known as the reindeer; on the American side of the water as the caribou. The two animals are specifically identical; but the latter are larger, heavier, stronger, and carry far finer antlers, which is probably due to better feeding and more extensive pasturage. Caribou appear to have been indigenous to Newfoundland, as may be surmised from the stone arrow-heads belonging to the aborigines of the island, which are occasionally found on the shores of the lakes, and could have been used for no other purpose than slaying deer. There is no doubt also that the island has been largely recruited from time to time from Labrador. Old settlers have told me that in severe winters, when the Straits of Belleisle have been frozen right across, they have seen large herds of deer crossing on the ice from the coast of Labrador, to the comparatively more genial climate of Newfoundland; and it is not likely they would ever return, if they could, seeing the magnificent pasturage they would find in their new home.

The habits and appearance of the caribou may be familiar to many sportsmen; to others they may not be so. It is to the latter I venture to address a few remarks, gathered principally from my own observation, and from that of Indians familiar with the subject.

In general appearance the caribou somewhat resembles a gigantic goat. The body is heavier and more clumsy than that of the red-deer; the legs are shorter and stouter, the feet broader, head more cow-like, eyes and ears smaller, and nostrils larger. The skin is brown in summer, brown and white in autumn, and white in winter; changing, in fact, with the seasons, like hares and ptarmigan. The hair is extremely thick and beautifully soft, having an under covering of soft warm wool, which gives it a springy touch, unlike the wiry hair of red-deer. The antlers of the caribou stag are palmated, sweeping backwards at first, and then forwards, and of magnificent proportions,—the brow-antlers sometimes meeting over the nose, like a pair of hands clasped in the attitude of prayer. More often they have one brow-antler fully developed, the other not. In all respects the animal is admirably provided to resist the inclement climates he is destined to inhabit; his short strong legs carry him over ground such as no horse could traverse, and his broad foot prevents him from sinking into the bogs or snow. A popular delusion is that the palmated horns of the caribou, especially the brow-antlers, are given him to scrape away the snow to reach the lichen upon which he feeds. In reality it is not so: the horns are given him on purpose for fighting; and the proof that they are not for scraping snow is clear from the fact that the deer *shed their horns when the snow is on the ground*, and all the winter through they have no horns: they scrape the snow with their nose, which is covered with hard skin on purpose, and with their feet. The stag is in his prime in September, and his horns are then at their full growth, clear of the velvet—in fact, "cleared for action"—and they shed them in November, after the rutting season. All this points to the conclusion that they are given them for fighting, and doubtless for ornament also.

During the rutting season, which commences about the third week in September, and lasts a fortnight, terrible battles take place; and it is rare to find a full-grown stag whose antlers are not battered, the brow-antlers especially, and the animal himself often badly bruised about the neck and shoulders. In defending themselves against wolves, they use their fore-legs with good effect. Unlike the rest of the deer tribe, the female caribou carries antlers, but not always. She brings forth her young in May, retaining her horns during the winter; the barren does shed theirs in winter. This would seem to be a provision of nature for the mother to be able to protect her young; and I have invariably noticed that an old doe with a fawn has got horns. A full-grown caribou hind is fully as large as a red-deer stag, and a full-grown caribou stag is half as large again.[1]

In coming to this conclusion I am not speaking at random, having killed both kinds many times. My experience of red-deer is that they average from fifteen stone upwards, and it is a very good stag that weighs twenty stone clean; whereas a caribou stag would average from twenty stone upwards, and thirty stone would be not at all an unusual weight.

From the inaccessible nature of the country the caribou inhabit, it is impossible to bring in the whole carcass and weigh it, as in Scotland. I have therefore been led to this conclusion by the general appearance of the animal, the size of its skin after preservation, the weight of its

---

[1] I use the words *doe* or *hind* indiscriminately. The Indians always speak of a *doe*. It ought, of course, to be *hind*, being the female of a *stag*. In the same way they speak of a *fawn* when it should be a *calf*. A *doe* and *fawn* only apply to fallow and small deer, when the male is a *buck*. The Indians also speak of an old caribou stag as an old "bull." "Moose" are spoken of as bull or cow, but I never heard of a *cow* caribou.

head, haunches, &c., when brought into camp. I have found it hard work with one Indian to even turn over a heavy stag; and after having been gralloched, skinned, quartered, the head cut off, and legs lopped off by the knee, it has taken four strong men to bring the meat into camp. Allowing 80 lb. for a load (an Indian considers 100 lb. a fair load), that would make 320 lb., less head, horns, paunch, skin, not counting a quantity of meat, such as the neck, saddle, &c., which they could not carry; I think, therefore, that I am not exaggerating when I reckon the beast clean at from 400 to 500 lb., and often more.

In habits caribou resemble the rest of the deer tribe; their vision I do not think is very acute, nor their hearing very wonderful; but like all the deer family, they trust entirely to their sense of smell, which is extraordinary. They have one peculiarity I have remarked, namely, of feeding *down* wind. This is very advantageous when stalking; and if the hunter can only get ahead of them and gain a good hiding-place, they will feed almost on the top of him; but if alarmed, they will turn up wind as soon as possible. They are not at any time difficult to stalk when once you have spied them, owing to the nature of the ground where they are generally found—amongst low juniper-bushes, the height of a man's head; but this also makes them difficult to spy, especially if lying down. Once seen, a certain shot may be generally obtained at almost any distance, with moderate precaution.

These deer, from being seldom hunted, have but little fear of man, so long as they don't wind him, and will often allow one to approach boldly; indeed, the big stags in the breeding season are much more inclined to fight than run away. The Indians can call or *tole*[1] them up within ten yards, if allowed to do so, but such a practice savours of butchery, and is unworthy of a sportsman; it is, however, often necessary to *tole* a big stag, to induce him to leave the hinds, and present a shot. When a stag is *toled*, he always tries to get to leeward of his enemy to get his wind, and the stalker

---

[1] *Toleing* the caribou is the reverse process to "calling" the moose. In the latter the cry of the female is imitated; in the former, the male. With the moose it is the poor brute's amatory feelings which are imposed on; with the caribou, his pugilistic ones.

CARIBOU-STALKING.

must prevent this at all hazards, even if he have to show himself; for if once the animal gets the least taint of wind, he is off like lightning, without wishing for further acquaintance. The hinds, as usual in these cases, always lead the van, the old stag bringing up the rear. *Toleing* is not difficult; all the Indians can do it with more or less success: the cry is a shuffling kind of grunt, altogether different from the roar of a red-deer stag.

The usual pace of a caribou is a long swinging trot if alarmed; but if the danger be imminent, they can gallop very fast. In galloping they make a clacking noise with their feet, caused by the toes being spread and coming together again. Their flesh is excellent. The stags are in their prime in August and September, when they have as much as five inches of fat on them. They run down very fast in the rutting season, during which time they eat nothing but sand and mud, and are of course unfit for food; at this time the hinds are in fine condition.

I have no doubt that caribou could be easily

domesticated in Newfoundland,[1] and made use of for draught purposes, as in Lapland. There is a portion of the island called the province of Avalon, connected with the main island by a narrow neck, part of which might be turned into a magnificent deer-park, and the deer preserved therein. This would at all events prevent them from being exterminated, as I fear they will be ere long, by the settlers, who go after them in the winter, when they are driven down from the barrens to the coast in search of food, and fire into the herd with their heavy seal-guns. In this way they kill numbers, and wound a great many more. I have killed stags with slugs in them. One butcher boasted that he had knocked down seven at a shot.

It is only fair to those who are contemplating a visit to Newfoundland, to tell them of the difficulties attending this sport. The first is the difficulty in getting to the ground, and the expense attached to the expedition. Newfoundland is, so far as the interior is concerned, un-

---

[1] I have since seen one, a young stag, in a farmhouse on the Cod Roy river. He came into the kitchen to be fed, like a dog. Another was caught and tamed by an Indian at Hall's Bay, but made its escape.

inhabited; consequently it is necessary to take everything with one, in the shape of provisions, tents, &c. This entails a number of men, who have also provisions to carry: the same men carry down the meat, unless it is proposed to leave it to rot upon the ground. It is necessary to have boats, to take your party and gear up the rivers, across lakes, &c., as there are no roads whatever; these boats must be light, to enable them to be poled up rivers, or transported across country, from one lake to another. For all this work Canadian lumberers are first-rate, being expert polers, handy axemen, and good at making a camp, or carrying a heavy load.

Provisions of all kinds can be obtained at St John's, from whence they would be conveyed along the coast by the coastal steamer: men and boats would have to be engaged beforehand. The amount of provisions and gear would be in accordance with the wants of the party: the principal items required are pork, flour, sugar, and tea, according to taste; the more gear the greater trouble, but, of course, greater comfort. A cooking-pot, kettle, and frying-pan are absolutely necessary; also warm clothes, and a good blanket or rug, as the nights are cold in September. One suit on, and one off, are sufficient, and two or three pairs of thick stockings, a stout pair of boots, a pair of moccasins, made by the Indians from the shanks of the first deer killed; guns and rifles complete the outfit, which will be found to occupy no little space. In addition to this, potted cocoa, or coffee and milk in tins, and compressed vegetables, add greatly to one's comfort; and of course pipes, tobacco, matches, candles, towel, soap, comb, tooth-brush, needles and thread, and a pair of binoculars, or stalking-telescope.

With regard to Indians, some people don't believe in them: I do. I have yet to learn what any sportsmen have done without Indians: they are thoroughly familiar with the country, and are experienced hunters and trappers, which the white men are not. The latter are very useful, but know nothing about deer-stalking, or the habits of the animals; in fact, the Indian represents the stalker, the white man the gillie: any one familiar with Scotch deer-stalking knows exactly what that means. The Indians have their faults; they are grasping and extortionate in their demands, and get sulky if not properly treated, or if a man won't work, or can't hit anything. But treat them liberally, with plenty to eat and not too much to drink, consult them on all matters connected with their calling, and I have always found them thoroughly up to their work, and most intelligent and amusing companions. I only speak from my own experience; and I would as soon go out after deer in that country without an Indian, as go to sea without a chronometer.

In the autumn of 1879, a party, consisting of two sportsmen, four Canadian lumberers, and a fine specimen of the British blue-jacket, started from the Bay of Islands, on the west coast of Newfoundland, on a caribou-hunting trip.

Two small boats loaded to the water's edge conveyed us and our traps to the mouth of the Humber, one of the finest rivers in the island, where the work of poling commenced.

The stream ran swiftly, with heavy rapids and eddying pools; but the men thoroughly knew their business, and, by taking advantage of eddies, with now and then a spell at the oars in slack water, maintained a steady average of three or four miles an hour against the current.

Two men, one in the bow, the other in the stern, are required for each boat, the principal work devolving upon the aftermost one, who, by bearing his whole weight upon the pole, keeps the boat steady whilst the foremost hand steers clear of boulders and snags; when fixing their poles simultaneously, away the slight craft dances over the foaming torrent.

After two or three hours of this work, we reached a "steady" or long stretch of slack water, where the oars were substituted for the poles, pipes lit, and yarns spun. Our "boss," a lean wiry backwoodsman, by name M'Cormack, was quite a character, and entertained us with his adventures in the woods, and his experience with the North American Indians, for whom he professed the most intense disgust. He seemed to have some reason for these feelings, since they badly used some of his family, and brutally treated his grandfather some years back; consequently, he related any retaliatory measures with much relish. One of the most satisfactory, in

DEER POND.

his opinion, was the introduction of smallpox, which decimated a whole tribe; but even that was eclipsed by a friend of his, who poisoned a well, and thus "wiped out" an entire colony. He seemed to think it quite a pity that some such remedy was not tried upon the Zulus, with whom we were then at war.

After several hours' poling, we reached the head of the river, eighteen miles from the mouth, and entered Deer Pond, a splendid sheet of water, nearly twenty miles long. After a short spell for refreshment, the oars were got out, and we paddled gaily along the tranquil surface of the lake. At this season of the year the shores of these lakes present a most beautiful appearance, the maples having already donned their autumnal tints of scarlet, green, and yellow, the colours being vividly reflected in the calm waters of the lake. The Humber river is especially beautiful in this respect; the stream winds through magnificent gorges, and the mountains, heavily timbered to their summits, rise to the height of 1500 feet on either side. Several kinds of pines, firs, hazels, birches, and maples adorn the banks;

but the pines are fast disappearing before the lumberer's axe. Salmon ascend the Humber in great numbers, and many seals follow them into the lakes of the interior. We reached our camping-ground about dusk, having traversed thirty-five miles since morning, mostly against the stream. Our men then set to work to pitch the camp, cut down trees, &c.; and in less than half an hour we were comfortably settled under our tent, before a roaring fire, composed of eight or ten fir-trees, over which the pot containing our dinner merrily hissed. Our beds, composed of the soft tops of the spruces cleverly arranged, were prepared for us, and after a glass of grog and a pipe, we soon coiled away for the night.

The next morning we were off early to examine some marshes at the back of our camp, where we hoped to find deer, but returned after a fatiguing tramp of several hours, having seen nothing; so, having breakfasted, we again took to the boats, and reached a farmhouse at the head of the lake by noon. The Humber river runs through Deer Pond, so we once more entered its waters, and after pulling another five miles,

Halt on the Portage—Humber River.

reached what is called in Newfoundland a portage or corduroy road through the woods, where we called a halt to make the necessary arrangements for dragging our boats across in the morning; but Cochrane and I pushed on, and camped for the night about half-way across. We found the portage to be nine miles, and knee-deep in mud the whole way, so that it was not till the next afternoon that we reached the shores of Grand Pond, a magnificent sheet of water at the far end.

The feelings awakened in the mind of an observer when sighting this beautiful lake for the first time, may be gathered from the following graphic description from the pen of the Rev. M. Harvey, who accompanied the governor across the island: "The shades of evening were closing as we got our first glimpse of Grand Lake, and a very beautiful and impressive sight it was. I sat down on the trunk of a pine-tree that had been washed up by the waves, and I gave myself up to the spirit of the hour and the influence of the scene. The shades of night had now darkened the hilltops, and only a stray breath of wind played on the surface of the lake. The stillness had in it something oppressive—almost painful. . . . To relieve this sombre mood, I tried to picture the good time coming, when the great valley, stretching from shore to shore, will be filled with a busy, prosperous population; when the forests will be cleared away and smiling cornfields and meadows will overspread the scene; when along the iron road will be gliding chariots of fire; when those blue waves will be the pathway for the steamboat with its tranquil motion; and when young men and maidens, old men and children, will mingle their voices here in songs of gladness." But with what different feelings does a sportsman regard these matters! To my mind the chief charm of the scene before me was its solitude; and if I had thought anything about it I should have said to myself, Here at least, in this peaceful spot, one can repose a while, undisturbed by the hum of a busy population. Those forests yet remain as God planted them; those hills have never yet been desecrated by the plough or the iron horse; nor those waters by the shrieking of the penny steamer conveying "'Arry" and his sweetheart on a picnic. Here is a spot where neither young men nor maidens, old men nor children, reside, and where tea-gardens and touters are unknown. The day will doubtless come when Grand Pond will be as hackneyed as Loch Katrine; when the air will reek with bad tobacco, and the hills re-echo the strains of a brass band, and the shores of that beautiful lake be strewn with empty bottles, old boots, and sardine-boxes; when those lovely woods will be cut down, and the hillsides and valleys ploughed up, drained, and planted; when the caribou and beaver will be extinct, and the Indians departed to the happy hunting-grounds. But I am not likely, nor do I wish, to see that time.

Whilst waiting the arrival of our baggage, we went to look for wild geese on the marshes, escorted by some miners who were exploring for coal in the neighbourhood.

We left our coats, rifles, cartridges, hunting-knives, and binoculars, hanging outside the miners' hut; and on our return, some hours afterwards, were horrified to find it in flames, and our property in great jeopardy. We saved the rifles and binoculars, but the clothes, pouches, and cartridges were destroyed. All the money I possessed was in the pocket of my shooting-coat, but we recovered it from the ashes when cooled down. It was fortunate our heavy baggage, with provisions, tent, &c., had not arrived.

The fire originated from a spark : the miners had been cooking their supper, and had incautiously neglected to put out the fire, although I had warned them about it.

Our boat and gear arrived after dark, the men being thoroughly done up with their day's work, so we camped on the borders of the lake, and the next morning launched our boats for the first time upon the waters of Grand Pond, the largest lake in Newfoundland, and after a very hard day's work, reached Sandy Point, a distance of thirty-five miles from the place of our departure, where we camped. This lake is sixty miles long. A large island divides it abreast of Sandy Point, leaving a narrow channel on either side, and it is at this point that the deer are in the habit of crossing later on in the year: already the sand on both sides was deeply impressed with their tracks, some of them quite fresh. Having an hour to spare before dark, we took our guns to try for a duck for our dinner, and had fired a few shots, when, to our astonishment, we heard a regular volley some distance down the lake in reply, and soon afterwards observed a canoe, with a solitary Indian approaching. The man told us that his family were beaver-hunting some way down the lake, and hearing our shots they fired a salute to give us a welcome; so the next morning we shifted our camp to where they were. We found them most comfortably established in a wigwam, beautifully constructed to keep out the wet. They said they had done pretty well with beavers, and the interior of the wigwam was festooned with skins, stretched out to dry. After considerable palaver, we engaged two of the Indians to pilot us to the barrens on the morrow.

The sun was high in the heavens the following day before our arrangements for the expedition were complete. Three days and a half had already elapsed since our departure, and not a living thing had we seen except a few ducks and mergansers, which we had shot coming up the river; but we now looked forward to getting some sport for our trouble, and the Indians assured us we should not be disappointed. The first thing to be done was to sort our baggage, leaving all the heavy gear, with the bulk of our provisions, down at the beach, with the boats, in charge of one of the party, who had orders to look out for deer crossing the water. The shores of the lake at the back of our camp rose at an angle of 45° for about 1500 feet, after which, we were informed, it was all plain sailing. Up this we had to go; so all being ready, we embarked and landed lower down, where a trail, known only to the Indians, led to the barrens above. A tall, powerful fellow, Levi by name, led the way, playfully wielding an axe to clear away any obstacles in the path, and carrying a load of 100 lb. on his back, the rest of the party following in single file, each man carrying a load according to his strength. After three hours' toil, and many spells, we reached the top, and hove to for refreshment. It was now about 2 P.M., and glad were we to throw down our packs and enjoy the fresh breeze and the glorious prospect before us.

We had now reached a plateau 1500 feet above the sea, from whence a fine panorama was obtained. Far as the eye could reach were open barrens, interspersed with clumps of firs, and lakes in all directions; looking back, and almost on a level with us, was Sir J. Glover's island. This island is twenty-five miles long; on the top of it is a lake, and in that lake another island, and in that island another lake,—and so on, like a Japanese puzzle-box. The general appearance of the country resembled a Scotch deer-forest, but with more wood and water. Under our feet the lichen, upon which the deer feed, grew thick; and from the numerous tracks leading in every direction, it was evident that we were in a perfect sanctuary for deer.

Our spirits rose accordingly: and once more shouldering our packs, we stepped gaily along, taking a bee-line for a clump of wood seven miles away, where the Indians proposed we should pitch our camp. They told us that not a white man had ever trod those barrens before, —a piece of information we were not sorry to learn, and M'Cormack christened the country "Kennedy's Plains" forthwith.

Suddenly, John Joe, who was leading, threw down his pack, and said he saw deer: devil a tail could we see! However, we took his word for it, and called a halt. The country hereabouts was covered with stunted junipers, so that we could not see far in any direction; but Joe said he had seen deer moving about amongst the bushes. Loading our guns and rifles, we followed him in that direction, and soon got sight of a fine young stag. Getting a fair broadside shot at him at 70 yards, I dropped him in his tracks, with a ball from the smooth-bore. The shot startled another deer, which Cochrane polished off in good style; and which proved to be a very fine hind,[1] with a better pair of horns than my stag. A pricket now made its appearance, running back, and gave me an easy shot with the "baby" express rifle; so that in less time than it has taken to record it, we had three deer down, and enough meat

---

[1] After the first day we shot no more hinds or young deer.

to keep us going for a week. This was a good beginning; and much pleased with our success, we made for camp, which we reached about sundown.

The next morning we were up betimes; and after a cup of coffee, started in opposite directions, John Joe going with me, and Levi with Cochrane. I must now tell my own story, since we were separated every day, only to meet in the evening.

Joe and I had walked for about a couple of hours, smoking and chatting about sport, &c., when the Indian stopped, and threw himself down, and I followed suit.

"I see deer," he said. We lay still for a while to survey the position, when a fawn fed out from behind a bush where he had been lying, not more than 60 yards off. He was presently followed by a hind, and then the antlers of a stag appeared. We dared not move, or the hind must have seen us; so we kept still till the stag fed into sight, when I fired and struck him fair behind the shoulder. To my disgust all three bolted, but the stag soon separated, showing he was badly wounded. We followed as hard as we could, but lost sight of him in a thickly wooded hollow, where he had lain down in the water, but sprang up not 20 yards off, when I gave him both barrels and rolled him over. After gralloching the stag—a fat beast, about the same size as the one I got the day before—we started again to examine some likely-looking ground to the southward; but, meeting with nothing there but a hind and a calf, we wheeled round so as to work homewards against the wind, when I saw in the distance a white object running along the hillside.

Pointing it out to Joe, he at once pronounced it to be a herd of deer, or "whole company" of them, as he expressed it, led by a white hind, with a very big stag bringing up the rear. My glasses proved him to be correct, for we counted seventeen or eighteen of them, in charge of a monster which loomed as big as a bullock, and carried a magnificent head. The deer were travelling diagonally towards us, down wind, so that by running as hard as we could for half a mile we were able to intercept their path, and had barely time to drop behind some low junipers before the leading hinds were upon us. It was an exciting moment as the graceful animals passed our ambush in twos and threes, some of them not more than five yards off, and none more than twenty. As they crossed our track, they winded it, jumped over, and, passing on, assembled themselves in our rear. Many of the hinds carried very fair antlers, and looked like stags. Joe was greatly excited, and kept whispering in my ear, "Take that one, sir; she got five inches of fat!" but I was deaf to his remarks, and kept my gun at half-cock; for I could hear the old bull grunting in rear of his harem. Presently his brow-antlers appeared — what a moment for a deer-stalker!—then his head and enormous neck—and what a pair of horns!—and then his huge carcass came in full view. Joe gave a grunt, the old brute stopped; and at that instant the heavy ounce-ball crashed in behind his shoulder, the poor brute gave a prodigious bound, clearing fifteen feet, as we afterwards measured, and then laid out at full gallop. I stood up and pulled the second trigger, but the cartridge missed fire: it mattered not, the gallant beast, going like a race-horse, but dying all the way, made straight for a lake, some 400 yards away, and plunging in, rolled over dead. Joe gave a grunt of satisfaction, and we forthwith "spliced the main-brace, drinking blood on the black knife," in Highland fashion. We then sat down to enjoy a pipe, and watch the hinds, which had scampered off at the shot, and now stood grouped a couple of hundred yards off, wondering what had become of their lord and master; but, not wishing to injure them, I fired a shot over their backs, sending them scampering off to look for another stag,— Joe's opinion being that they would not be long before they had found one, as other stags are always following the hinds at this season, and are only deterred from joining the herd by the presence of a bigger and stronger stag than themselves. We now proceeded to drag the old fellow out of the lake, which was, fortunately, a shallow one. His horns stuck up out of the water like a branch of a tree. After a good deal of trouble we got him ashore, and surveyed his noble proportions. "He very ole stag," said Joe: "about ten year ole, and weigh over 500 lb." But, by Jove, what a head!—forty-two points, as I'm a sinner! with the palmated brow-antlers interlocked across his nose, like a pair of clasped hands, his huge bull-neck and shoulders bearing many a scar, gained in defence of his seraglio. I named him "Brigham Young" on the spot, out of compliment to the Mormon elder; and his grand old head looks sadly on me as I write the account of his death. Ah, well! his end was peace—and a very tough piece he proved to be!

Having performed the last offices to Brigham, we shouldered his head, at least Joe did, for I don't think I could have carried it, and returned to camp, which we reached at 1 P.M. The first thing that met our eyes was a splendid stag's head, propped up against a tree, showing that Cochrane had also been successful, and had gone out again; so after a hasty meal, Joe and I did likewise, but we saw no more deer that day. On our return to camp at sundown we found Cochrane just come in; he had met with another big stag in the afternoon, and badly wounded it, but lost it. We had not done badly, however—over six deer in a day and a half; so we spent a very merry evening over our pipes and grog, and turned in at peace with all the world.

The next day being Sunday, was observed as a day of rest, at least as far as we were concerned; but with six deer lying out in different directions, some of them nine miles from camp, it was necessary to bring in the meat; so all hands went out for that purpose, and returned in the evening, bearing huge quarters of venison, heads, skins, &c., all of which we triced up to the trees round the camp, presenting a very picturesque and sporting appearance. The quantity of meat attracted a number of moose-birds, a species of jay, which became so impudent, and pecked the meat so badly, that we had to make an example of some of them. Our party were now in high spirits, with plenty to eat and to drink, fine weather, and good sport; in fact, we might have kept a ship's company with food if we had only had them up there. Ptarmigan were plentiful, but so tame we seldom molested them, except to knock over a brace or so for the pot; wild-fowl were also numerous. The Indians were very well satisfied with our success, of which they were not a little proud; and well they might be, for without them we should have got nothing. We found the big stags rather tough, so we lived on the hind and pricket; but M'Cormack was rash enough to try "Brigham's" tongue, and pronounced it mighty strong.

On Monday morning Cochrane and I changed stalkers, Joe going with him and Levi with me. We left the camp at daylight after a cup of coffee, but unwisely taking no food with us, as we felt certain of killing a stag for breakfast. My coxwain, the blue-jacket before-mentioned, begged to be allowed to come also. We walked for four hours over hill and dale, forest and swamp, without seeing anything, and we began to think our breakfast would be of the lightest, when Levi said he saw deer in a wood. For the life of me I could not make out anything, even with my glasses; but these Indians have such wonderful eyesight that I felt perfectly confident; so we made a long detour to get to leeward of the place.

From some high ground above we could look down the valley; and there, sure enough, were the deer—nine of them, some feeding, some lying down—in a lovely secluded spot. It was almost a pity to disturb them; but a hungry man has no compunction. We could make out one good stag, if not two; but the small stags and hinds, being both antlered, are not easily distinguished from each other. To reach the spot was no easy matter, the valley being only open from below; the wind was from that direction, and all round the top and sides were densely wooded. We had therefore to crawl down through the wood to get a shot; and entering at the point nearest to where the deer were feeding, we managed to crawl down, avoiding dry twigs and rotten windfalls, till we got within shot of a small stag and some hinds. Leaving my coxwain at this place, I crawled on with the Indian till we saw a good stag below us; the deer was standing broadside at seventy or eighty yards—a splendid chance, but for a bush which covered his shoulder completely. I waited till he fed clear, when he turned quarter-face to me; when, aiming for the point of the shoulder, I fired. Simultaneously came the report of my coxwain's rifle, and I saw his stag roll over. Not so mine, as he bolted with the rest; but feeling sure he was hit, we followed, and soon saw him separate from the hinds and walk slowly down the valley, evidently very sick. We came up with him after a chase of half a mile, when I finished him. The stag was a well-grown beast of about four years old, very fat, but not much of a head. The first ball had struck the point of the shoulder and passed out on the opposite flank.

We soon lit a fire, and by eleven o'clock were breakfasting off grilled kidneys roasted on a stick. The meat proved most excellent — although, for the matter of that, we were so hungry we would have eaten it raw. A hind watched our proceedings from a neighbouring hillock; but leaving her unmolested, we skinned the deer, and shouldering as much meat as we could carry, returned home, where Cochrane had already arrived, having also killed a stag about the same size as mine.

John Joe now said he wanted to examine his beaver-traps, a day's journey to the southward; so as we didn't care to go with him, we took a spell whilst the men were bringing in the meat, stretching the skins, or otherwise employed about the camp. Our provisions were getting short; no tea, sugar, or whisky left, and "baccy" scarce, but abundance of meat and biscuit still remaining; so we decided to go out for one more stalk, and then make tracks, as we had as much meat as we cared for or could carry. Joe having returned, came with me, and Levi with Cochrane, as on the first day. Joe told me that whilst on his way to his traps he met with a big stag. He was not looking for deer, and did not want to kill him, but the stag went for him. He threw stones, or, as he called it, rocks at him, but the beast still came on; so he shot it in the neck, at six paces, with small shot, and killed it. This may sound an improbable yarn to any one unacquainted with the audacity and fierceness of stags in the rutting season. I was not anxious to kill any more deer, so we went to have a look at this stag. We had walked for seven miles without seeing anything except a brood of grouse, out of which I bagged three brace, when we saw an enormous beast on the opposite side of a valley. He looked fully as big as "Brigham," and carried a splendid head, so we proceeded to stalk him. Crossing the valley we ascended the opposite hill, and on reaching the sky-line, saw our big friend, accompanied by several hinds and a small stag, which kept at a respectful distance. This small fellow gave us a deal of trouble, as he was feeding between us and the rest, so that we could not approach without giving him our wind; but by taking advantage of a hollow in the ground, we got within 100 yards of the master of the herd. I could not, however, get a shot, owing to some bushes which screened him; we therefore kept quiet, watching our chance. Meanwhile the young one, quite unconscious of danger, fed up to within five yards of where we lay. I had half a mind to put a ball through his head and take my chance at the old one, when, to our relief, he fed away and disappeared round a hummock. It was bitterly cold, the sleet falling on us all this time, and we were much cramped, so Joe suggested a "call" to bring up the big stag. And now a most laughable scene occurred. Joe commenced grunting, rolling his head from side to side, and bringing the sound out of his stomach as it seemed. The effect was magical. At the first grunt the stag tossed his head, faced about, roared back a challenge, and cleared for action. Another series of grunts from Joe, and the stag advanced, stamped his foot, rattled his horns against a tree, as though saying, "Who's afraid? Come on! I'm ready for you. I was laughing at the ridiculous sight, but shivering with cold at the same time. Hearing the challenge, but seeing nothing, the stag now moved cautiously forward, and turned broadside to catch the direction of the sound. At that instant I "let him have it," when, to my dismay, the whole lot bolted, the stag bringing up the rear. They stopped for a moment on the sky-line, looked back, and then disappeared as though they meant to put a few miles between us ere they pulled up.

"You missed him, sir," was all Joe said. Yes, Joe, I'm afraid I did; 'twas the cold that did it! However, as soon as their sterns disappeared over the sky-line, we were up and after them, but with little hopes of ever seeing them again. On reaching the top, very much pumped, Joe's quick eye caught a glimpse of them trotting quietly along, so we went on their tracks. I was fast dropping astern when Joe cried out that they had turned, and were coming right down towards us. To drop behind a bush was the work of an instant, when the leading hind came in sight, cautiously picking her steps, with ears cocked forward to catch the slightest sound. She passed where we were lying, not twenty paces off; the rest followed, with the big stag bringing up the rear. Joe hurriedly whispered, "You hit him, sir; see, his belly covered with blood!" I had but time to notice that it was so, when he was abreast of us, and a ball from the smooth-bore crashed through his shoulder, followed by another through the ribs. The stag plunged wildly forward, and after staggering a few yards, pitched head-foremost into the bracken. Joe gave several grunts of great satisfaction, and I slapped him on the back and congratulated him on as fine a piece of stalking as ever I saw,[1] for without his aid I should never have

---

[1] The last time I saw poor Joe he was at his own home in Hall's Bay, dying, I fear, of consumption.

taken the trouble of following up the deer after the first shot. Our stag, which we named "Joe Smith," after another Mormon elder, from having so many wives, proved a noble specimen, fully as heavy as his brother "Brigham," and counting thirty-six points on his antlers, which were widespread and beautifully shaped. On examining him we found the first shot, when we thought I had missed him, had struck him too low down, and passing through the body, had carried with it a lump of fat as big as my fist, which had plugged the hole and stopped the bleeding on that side; hence his indifference to the wound, which must eventually have caused his death.

Cutting off J. Smith's head, we turned our faces homewards, Joe bearing the trophy aloft on his shoulders—on our way to camp meeting with another fine stag with three hinds; but satisfied with my day's sport, I would not molest them. We passed the deer Joe had killed two days before, and stopped to admire its head, a very pretty one, and then without further adventure reached camp.

The next day we struck our camp; and the

same evening, after a very heavy day's work, reached the shores of Grand Pond, where we had left our boat. During our absence only one deer had crossed the water, a hind, and she was shot; so that would have been the extent of our sport had we preferred that style of shooting as recommended to me by a noble sportsman in St John's; whereas, by hard work and fair stalking, we had killed ten good stags and a hind in five days.

Not much more remains to be told. We were detained for three days by a north-east gale, which raised a heavy sea on the lake; but at last, losing all patience, Cochrane and I crossed in a canoe with two Indians, and ascending a fearfully stiff mountain on the further side, we took a bee-line across country and reached the ship on the second day.

Just as we left the beach, we saw a beautiful stag come out of the wood, with the apparent intention of crossing the lake; but winding our footsteps he turned back, and disappeared into the wood again. We might easily have shot him, but preferred to let him enjoy life, being satisfied with our success,

Camp on Grand Pond.

and having no pleasure in killing for killing's sake.

The boats with our gear and trophies arrived two days after us, and so ended a most enjoyable excursion. We parted with our Indians with regret. They had served us faithfully and well, so we loaded them with good things to take back to their camp; and before leaving the ship, I sent them down to get a good square meal, telling my steward to give them all they wanted, and adding that one of them was a teetotaller! They appeared long afterwards looking very comfortable; and in answer to my inquiries the steward remarked, "Well, sir, this one drank a bottle of whisky and a bottle of sherry! the teetotaller drank eight bottles of beer! and they polished off ten pounds of meat between 'em!"

I may mention here that none of the meat which we had left upon the ground was wasted, for during our delay at Grand Pond we sent the men up to the barrens and brought it down. Even if we had not done so, the Indians said they would use it all up.

On our overland journey back to the ship, we had a sample of the wonderful "instinct," if one may say so, with which Indians will find their way across an unknown country. One of them, John Joe, had never been on that ground; the other had once, but long ago. We travelled all day through woods, marshes, and barrens, with no trail or anything to guide us that we could see, but there was never any hesitation or doubt in their minds. It was coming on dark, and the leading Indian said we must make a camp for the night, as we could go no further. He had previously told us there was a "tilt" (a kind of wigwam) about half-way to the bay, which we hoped to reach before dark. "Why not go on?" I said. "Too dark," he replied. "Could you find your way without us, if you were alone?" "Yes." "Then go on,"—and go on we did; and the first thing we met, after stumbling through a thick wood, in utter darkness, was the wigwam, about three feet off. The Indians made us very comfortable in it; and as our provisions were exhausted, they supplied us from their store, baking most excellent bread, cooking our food, and boiling water to make tea in a cup made out of birchbark,[1] stripped from the nearest tree! No wonder I speak well of these Indians; they would live in the woods, and thrive where a white man would starve. I shall have more to say of them later on.

[1] Curiously enough, the bark does not burn, the water inside preventing it.

Brigham Young.

CHAPTER XI.

SECOND EXPEDITION AFTER CARIBOU—1880.

We must now suppose a year to have elapsed since the adventures in the last chapter were recorded.

Exactly at the same time of year—to a day, in fact—the Druid happened to be anchored in the same spot where she had been in 1879. The fishery season was practically over, and her engines were being overhauled preparatory to her summer flight to warmer latitudes. Taking advantage of these fortuitous circumstances, a party, of which I was a member, started on a second expedition into the interior of the island. My companion, Cochrane,[1] who had been with me

---

[1] Lieutenant Thomas Cochrane, then a sub-lieutenant in the Druid.

on the former occasion, again accompanied me. A keen sportsman and boon companion, always good-tempered, ready for anything, be the weather wet or dry, the provisions scarce or plenty, the liquor short or abundant, I could wish for no better or more cheery companion. Besides ourselves, was a connection of my own, whose great ambition was to slay the lordly caribou on his native barrens, for which purpose he had come out expressly from England. On this occasion we had no fewer than seven white men to carry our gear, necessitating two light boats and a larger one. This big boat gave us no end of trouble and anxiety; and we had a hard job to track her past a notorious rapid, near the head of the Humber river, called the " Devil's Dancing-hole,"—a very appropriate name, judging by the infernal current (running fourteen knots an hour), and the whirlpool caused by the same. After a laborious day's work, we reached the head of Deer Pond about midnight, and availed ourselves of the kind hospitality of a farmer and his wife, who had settled in this solitary spot. The next day we crossed the portage with the usual difficulties, and camped once more on the shores of Grand Pond, where we fell in with the telegraph repairer, a Mr Squires, who gave us a hearty welcome to his hut.

Whilst we were having our supper in this place, a weasel came in and endeavoured to drag away a hare which was lying in the hut; nor would he desist until Lyon killed him with his hunting-knife. I mention this because these vermin are usually so shy: this little rascal had apparently no fear of man. Our party was now reinforced by three Indians and an Indian woman—Levi, John, Reuben-Soulian, and Mrs Reuben. Crossing the lake in a storm of wind and rain, we camped for the night on the south side, wet through and very miserable, and the next morning started for the barrens,— every one, Mrs Reuben included, loaded to the utmost with provisions and gear. After a most fatiguing climb we reached the plateau, and pitched our camp in a swamp; in fact there seemed no choice, as the whole country was under water. In the afternoon we went stalking, but not expecting to see deer in such a place; nevertheless we did meet with three, in the evening, crossing the swamp to some high barrens in the distance. Reuben, by running, managed to cut them off, and with a wonderfully lucky shot, put a ball through the head of a young stag.

The next day we shifted our camp to higher and drier ground, selecting a desirable site in a small belt of wood, about eight miles from our former position. The country traversed was knee-deep in water the whole way, and the labour of transporting the baggage and provisions for so large a party was severe; but all shared in the work, making light of difficulties —the Indian woman carrying a load upon her back which would have shamed a London porter. After a short spell for rest and refreshment, we ascended a steep hill at the back of our camp, and at last found ourselves on dry barrens, with deer-tracks leading in all directions. We now separated, Reuben going with Cochrane, John with Lyon, and Levi accompanied me. The two former were fortunate in meeting with a whole "company" of deer, out of which Cochrane killed a fine stag and missed another, and Lyon distinguished himself by knocking over a stag at full gallop at 120 yards. I saw nothing, though I met with fresh tracks. On my way home we came across a beaver-dam, beautifully constructed, but the animals were not at home; probably the sound of the axe, where the men were cutting up firewood, had caused them to retire to safer quarters till the danger was past. These animals are very abundant in Newfoundland, and if protected in the breeding season they will be so for years to come. It would be a sad pity if they were allowed to be exterminated; and I always tried to impress this upon the Indians for their own interests, if for no other reason.[1] The beaver is far and away the most intelligent little animal on the face of the earth, and nothing will convince me but that he has been gifted by the Creator not only with instinct, but with reasoning powers. All his actions point to this. He generally selects the site for his abode on the banks of a small stream, and having built his house, he proceeds to dam up the stream below. To do this he has to select trees growing near the bank suitable for the purpose, which he cuts

[1] A law has since been passed to protect this useful and valuable little animal.

down with his teeth in such a manner as to cause them to fall across the stream. He has to calculate the force of the current, and build his dam in such a way as to withstand it, as well as any weight of ice that may come down; therefore it is built arched, with the convex side upstream. He *must* know the consequence of damming up the stream—that it will cause the water to rise, and so protect his habitation. All this is not mere instinct, but *reason* pure and simple; and my opinion is, that the beaver has far more intelligence and common-sense, if not reasoning powers of a higher order, than half the worthless scum who pursue him with such unrelenting and senseless pertinacity. The flesh of the beaver is excellent, but rather rich; and the tail is a most dainty morsel.

On returning to camp we found the lumberers had worked hard. Our tent, neatly pitched on rising ground, looked the picture of comfort, with nice dry beds of soft spruce-boughs neatly arranged, and covered with a waterproof sheet. A roaring fire in front gave out a glowing heat; and from the iron pot, suspended from a bent stick stuck in the ground, came forth the delicious steam of well-cooked venison-steaks. A pile of fir-logs, to last the night, showed that the Canadian axemen had done their work well. Nor was the comfort of our honest companions neglected, a most comfortable "lean-to" having been provided for themselves, and the Indians having erected a "tilt" for their own accommodation. Our wet clothes hung suspended from a line; the faithful Norris, my coxwain, had oiled and cleaned the rifles, which were stacked against a tree, the firelight dancing on their well-burnished barrels. Altogether a more perfect picture of camp-life could not be imagined.

The rain had ceased, and the moon shed her soft light through the lofty firs, the only sound to break the stillness of the night being the occasional weird cry of the loon from the distant lake. Our simple but substantial repast concluded, pipes are filled, the glass goes round, yarns are spun, and sounds of merriment resound from the lumberers' camp, amidst which we can detect the cheery strains of "Tom Bowling,"[1] or the "Lass that loves a sailor." The

---

[1] We had two brothers of the name of Bowling with us, and one of them was Tom.

rapturous applause ceases, we roll ourselves in our blankets, and in a few moments the camp is as silent as the grave.

The next morning, after our ablutions in the burn, and a hearty breakfast — for we have grown wiser by experience — we slowly wound our way up the steep pitch behind the camp to the hunting-grounds above. We had not gone a mile from the top before deer were reported, and a small stag responded to the call. As I had not killed anything, he was told off to me, and I put a ball into him, just to show "there's no ill feeling." The stag took the hint and absconded, and I after him, firing as I ran. This deer had a strong objection to parting with his life, and I put five bullets into him before he succumbed, and fell over into a lake, out of which we speedily dragged him.

Judge of my disgust at finding his body all covered with warty excrescences, presenting a loathsome appearance. I at first thought he must have been badly wounded by slugs: the Indian said it was done fighting; but this I could not believe, because a small stag, as he was, would never stand up to be so shamefully gored by a bigger one.

M'Cormack thought it was a disease, resembling farcy, to which he said cows were liable—and I think he must be right; anyhow, we left the carcass where it lay. The wretched little beast need not have been so particular about saving his life; in fact, he ought to have been grateful to me for putting an end to his miserable existence.

The same afternoon I fell in with Cochrane; and while we were having our lunch together, we saw a fine young stag coming leisurely our way. Levi and I started to cut him off; and I am bound to say the Indian made a mess of it, for he brought me close to the stag, certainly, but to windward, and the deer bolted. Cochrane, however, got him soon afterwards. On the way home we inadvertently gave three deer our wind. It was no one's fault, as they were lying down; but there was a whopping big stag amongst them, which was vexatious.

Altogether this day's work was very unfortunate, and I was not very well pleased with the performance. Lyon had been successful, and had killed a stag; so we had all three got something, such as it was! The next day it blew a gale of wind, and was bitterly cold. We now changed Indians—Reuben-Soulian falling to me, which I was not sorry for, as I had reason to believe he was a good stalker, and I had no great confidence in the others. Reuben and I stepped briskly along to keep ourselves warm, for the wind was cruelly cold, and traversed some likely-looking valleys, well sheltered, with plenty of wood and water, but no deer were there. By noon we had been walking five hours without seeing a beast, so we then turned up-wind. It had been on our beam so far; and on reaching the top of a hill, our eyes were gladdened by the sight of seven or eight hinds and a young stag, with one splendid fellow in charge of the party. The deer were close below us, feeding down-wind, according to their habit, so we hid behind some junipers, and waited their approach. The young stag— a three-year-old one—as usual kept his distance from the herd, for if ever he closed, down went the old one's head, and away he scampered. This foolish young fellow presently came close to where we were lying, and at once saw us, but not getting our wind, didn't know what to make of us; so he stood there, half-a-dozen yards off, eyeing us inquisitively. Reuben wanted me to shoot him, fearing he would give the alarm, and spoil the chance at the big one, who was now advancing and chasing the hinds about; but I would not do so, but tried to drive him away by speaking to him and waving my handkerchief. This he took no notice of; so, disregarding him, I ran forward to get a shot at the old "bull." Getting a view of his flank, I gave him the first barrel of my rifle, and the second as he slewed round to go. One of the shots took effect—I cannot say which in the excitement of the moment; so dropping my rifle, I took the smooth-bore from Reuben, and fired at the biggest of the herd as they went by me at full gallop.

Reuben, who had kept his eye on the big stag, said he was lying dead. We found that only one of the bullets had struck him, but that was in the right place, and clean through. He was a splendid beast, with a noble pair of antlers of thirty-eight points. The remarkable feature in his head was that he had only one brow-antler, but that one was a whopper, reaching down to the tip of his nose, and more than a foot in breadth. We gralloched the stag, cut off his head, and skinned him, so that his own mother would not have known him; and having packed as much on our backs as we could carry, were starting for camp, when, glancing back, I saw another deer lying dead, which proved to be the young one who had inspected us, and whose life I had previously spared. The heavy ounce ball had gone right through him, and the deer must have fallen dead in his tracks, but a bush prevented me from seeing it. This stag was in splendid condition, and must have scaled fully eighteen stone; his head did not amount to much. The old stag would be about 500 lb., and it was as much as Reuben and I could do to turn him over. On nearing camp we met Cochrane, who had killed two splendid stags with very fine heads, one of which Levi was carrying on his shoulders.

The following morning I left camp early, with Reuben and the two men, to bring in the deer killed the day before—my companions, Cochrane and Lyon, dispersing in different directions. We walked five or six miles, and were in sight of the dead stags, when Reuben spotted three deer—a stag, hind, and a fawn—about a mile off, so we ran across a marsh to cut them off, and succeeded in doing so. Reuben "toled" up the stag—a fine fellow, but not so big as the largest I had killed the day before,—and he gave me a grand chance at not more than 50 yards; but thinking I was sure of him, I waited for him to turn broadside, as he was then facing me, when he suddenly wheeled round, and made off after the hind and calf. I got a snap-shot at 100 yards, and heard the crack of the ball; but they all went off at a gallop, and disappeared over the sky-line. We noticed that the stag appeared to be making heavy weather of it, and could hardly keep up; but some other deer coming up, took off our attention. There was no stag amongst this lot; so I gave the rifle to my coxwain to try his hand, and he badly wounded a hind at fully 200 yards, but lost her. We then left the men to skin and quarter the deer killed the day previously, whilst Reuben and I went on. Soon after we had left the party, an immense stag passed close to them; but having no weapon, they were forced to let him alone. Meanwhile Reuben and I stepped gaily along, meeting with several hinds and calves, when suddenly a wounded stag passed close in front of us, and before I could get the rifle out of the cover had disappeared. We recognised the one I had fired at in the morning, by his horns as well as by the hind and calf that accompanied him. I sent the Indian to try and cut him off; but he was unable to do so, although he got close enough to see the blood on his side. I would rather have missed him clean; but these accidents will happen in deer-stalking as in all kinds of shooting. We were now in the heart of a very sporting-looking country, scattered over with woods, marshes, and juniper; so we climbed up on a rock to spy the ground, and Reuben soon saw a big stag walking along by himself, about two miles off. We were thinking of trying to circumvent him, when we heard three shots to windward; the big stag also heard them, and took the hint, moving off down-wind, so we turned our faces towards home, nine miles off, and reached camp without further adventure. The three shots we heard came from Lyon, who had killed an enormous stag, but with a very poor head— his horns having been apparently knocked all to pieces in fighting.

We had now plenty of meat in camp, but a great many mouths to feed; for thirteen men will consume a good many pounds of meat in a day, especially when working hard as we were. Reuben's wife proved most useful, and well earned her dollar a-day, which we voted her, although she expected nothing. She mended our clothes, made our moccasins, cooked our dinner, baked us most excellent bread, and was altogether a great acquisition. The weather was fine, provisions abundant, and game plentiful— what more could a man want? It is true that our whisky began to run short, and had to be economised; we had brought up a good supply for our party, but under the belief that two-thirds of them were teetotallers, as they represented themselves to be. I am bound to say, however, with all due respect for that most excellent order, that after the first day's work there was only one teetotaller left, the rest of them coming for their grog as regularly as cows to be milked; and I think they were all the better for it.

We had up to this time killed eleven stags, and we all agreed that one more to make up the dozen would be a fair bag. Our score stood thus: Lyon three, Cochrane four, myself three, and Reuben one; so this day we went out stalking for the last time. It was a pretty dense fog when we reached the top of the ascent leading to the barrens, and we soon lost sight of each other; Reuben and I steered, as far as we could judge, for the rock from whence we had spied the stag the evening before. The fog was wet and raw, and the wind blew bitterly cold across the barrens, so we had to step out smartly to keep ourselves warm, hoping that the fog would lift. And so it did: suddenly the curtain rose, unveiling as lovely a scene as ever sportsman beheld. Far as the eye could reach were mountains and valleys, lakes, woods, and rocks; conspicuous among the last the "Lobster House"[1] reared its head. Probably a finer

---

[1] A remarkable rock, so called, I conclude, because there is not a lobster within 100 miles of it, nor a house within forty.

panorama could not be seen in Newfoundland than that obtained from this neighbourhood. Standing, as we were, in the middle of the island, an uninterrupted view could be had for fifty miles in every direction. To the north-west, the mountains in the vicinity of Bonne Bay were plainly visible; looking eastward were the " White Hills " around Hall's Bay, with Sandy Pond and other fine lakes apparently at our feet. The chain of mountains forming the southern boundary of Grand Pond,[1] stretched away to the western horizon, and with my glasses I could see the glittering waters of that glorious lake. The southern horizon was broken by the mountains surrounding Red Indian Lake, a noble sheet of water thirty-seven miles long; and I believe from where we stood the sea might be seen on both sides of the island on a clear day.

Near us were marshes, ponds, and scattered clumps of wood, a very sanctuary for deer and beaver, and a glorious prospect for a deer-

---

[1] Grand Pond is 56 miles long, and has an area of 192 miles; this, however, includes an island over 20 miles long, leaving the area of water 136 square miles—a tidy-sized " pond."

stalker; not a soul or a human habitation to be seen, nor a sound heard except the crow of an old cock grouse, or the more distant cry of the loon. The beautifully variegated lichen afforded soft and elastic walking for our moccasined feet, and the hares scarcely deigned to get up out of our way as we passed by. About noon we reached the rock from which we had spied the deer the evening before; and Reuben climbed up to have a look round while I had my luncheon under the lee. Presently Reuben cried out, "I see him—very big stag; regular ole bull—I tink same as we see yesterday; there he is a mile off, coming our way." Cramming the remains of my frugal repast into my pocket, we loaded the gun and rifle, and went to cut him off, in high spirits. In a very few minutes we were ahead of him, and paused to take breath under a juniper.[1] The stag was a fine fellow, evidently an old warrior, who had been beaten off by some bigger stag, and very sulky he looked in consequence, and very vicious also. When about 200 yards off, Reuben gave a grunt: the stag threw up his head and

---

[1] In reality a larch, but called juniper in Newfoundland.

challenged back, coming boldly forward ready for another fight. Seeing nothing, he edged down to leeward to get the wind; but this we could not allow, so we moved out into the marsh to prevent it. We were now in full view of the stag, who came forward again snorting defiance; but not trusting his eyesight, he again edged off to get to leeward. Now was the moment, his broad flank was exposed, and a ball from the smooth-bore crashed through his shoulder, followed by another within six inches of the first. The poor beast turned, staggered, and endeavoured to make off, but too late. Dropping the gun, I seized the rifle, and the stag rolled over, with three bullets through his body. This animal had evidently been fighting hard; his horns, which were very fine ones, were much knocked about, and his neck and shoulders badly wounded. We cut off his head and skin, and got back to camp soon after dark. My companions had not been successful; but Lyon had killed a good barren hind, making our bag twelve stags and one hind. The next day we brought in the meat and prepared for a start, and the following morning struck our camp, and reached the shores of Grand Pond the same evening, after a heavy day's work.

Those of my readers who have followed me so far, and are not quite exhausted with the somewhat monotonous details of deer-stalking, may care to follow me in a third expedition, which differed slightly from the last, inasmuch as we struck in from the east side of the island instead of the west as in the preceding years. In both cases we reached the same high barrens where the deer love to congregate; and, as a matter of fact, our camp of 1881 was only twenty miles from, and almost in sight of, our camping-ground of 1880.

Although the incidents connected with deer-stalking must necessarily be somewhat similar, there are always details in every stalk different from another. I therefore relate them, perhaps too minutely, exactly as they occurred. If to any they afford as much pleasure in reading as they do to myself in relating, I shall be well satisfied.

CHAPTER XII.

THIRD EXPEDITION AFTER CARIBOU.

Towards the end of the year 1881, as the Druid steamed up Halls' Bay, one of the magnificent estuaries on the east coast of Newfoundland, a solitary Indian might have been observed standing on the shore, with his little dog, eagerly watching the ship as she passed on to her anchorage.

I fancied somehow I had seen that figure before, also the little dog, so I presently landed, and found my old friend Reuben, who had walked over from the Bay of Despair, on the south coast where he lived, on the chance of picking us up. "Well, captain," said he, "I'm glad to see you. I was afraid you were never coming." I thought the poor fellow looked rather thin. He told me he had walked across in eight days and had been without food for four of them. The distance is not, perhaps more than 100 miles as the crow flies, but equal to at least four times that length owing to the woods, swamps, and rivers one would have to cross.

There is one thing about an Indian, he can go without food for days, and then gorge himself with a cargo sufficient to last him a week, like a dog.

It so happened that we had to wait for the Fantôme at an appointed rendezvous near Hall's Bay, so that Reuben's arrival was most opportune, and we arranged for a few days' hunting without delay. We managed to secure the services of one of the numerous Joe family—a tall raw-boned Indian of immense strength. Poor John Joe was too ill to come, and I fear that he has already succumbed to the disease which is slowly but surely killing off his race.[1]

Our party on this occasion consisted of three sportsmen—Sir Rose Price, Baird, and myself—the two Indians, two blue-jackets, and a couple

[1] Consumption.

of lumberers, hard working and willing fellows, who well earned their five shillings a-day.

The usual difficulties beset us on starting: rivers too low for poling, a gale of wind on the lake, camping with all our gear soaked, and when at last we reached dry land, a tedious tramp through burnt woods for ten miles; so that it was not till noon of the third day after leaving the ship that we reached our destination, and pitched our camp in the middle of an extensive marsh. After a short spell to straighten our backs, we started off in different directions to try and get some venison for supper. Reuben and I had not left the camp a quarter of an hour, when, looking back, we saw a fine stag come out of the wood and proceed leisurely across the marsh down-wind. We had a sharp run back through the woods to get ahead and to leeward of him; and I had just time to drop behind a stone in the marsh, and get my wind, when the stag approached and gave me a fine shot at about seventy yards. The sharp crack of the ball told that the old Scotch rifle had done its work well, but the deer bolted across the marsh at a gallop. I stood up and gave him the other barrel, striking him on the flank; but this seemed only to quicken his pace, and he disappeared round a belt of wood. The country hereabouts was marshy, with clumps or *drogues* of wood scattered about like islands in a sea. We followed the direction the deer had gone in but saw nothing of him, and it was impossible to follow his track in the marsh, as it was knee-deep in water. Much disgusted, I went back to the stone, stepped the distance, looked for blood, but could find none, and I had almost given up the stag as lost, when Reuben called out to me that he had found the trail, with drops of blood, leading across a small brook. I now sent him back to camp, not 500 yards off, to fetch his little dog, whilst I waited, taking care not to disturb the trail. On his way to camp, Reuben met with another stag, and fired three shots at it, but without effect. I saw the deer coming my way, bounding over the low bushes, and I was all ready to receive him, when he turned and went off another way, having doubtless winded our footsteps crossing the marsh.

Reuben soon returned; when following up

the blood-trail we came upon the stag lying dead. Both bullets had passed clean through his body—the first right in the middle of his carcass, the second diagonally. How he could have travelled so far is a marvel, but it shows how tenacious of life are these deer. The stag was in first-rate condition, and carried a good head.

Soon afterwards my companions returned, one having killed a young stag, the other a hind; so we had a good supper of liver and bacon and grilled kidneys. The next day two of us went stalking and one remained in the camp, as it seemed a first-rate pass for deer. The Baronet took a southerly direction and killed a small stag; I saw nothing till returning home, when we met with a stag, hind, and calf crossing the marshes. We managed to cut them off, and I wounded the stag, which tottered across the marsh and then lay down, and ought to have been bagged easily; but, sending two Indians round, I made too sure of him, and went across the marsh to finish him, when he suddenly sprang up and made off, on three legs, at a gallop, and passing close to one of the

Indians, who missed him, in fine style, disappeared in the woods, and darkness coming on, was lost. This event did not concern me greatly, as he was not a big stag; but I was sorry to have wounded the poor creature, and to have lost him stupidly after all.

The next day Baird killed a fine big stag with a good head; and as it was his first one, he was very much pleased, and related the details of the stalk with great excitement. I travelled over a good deal of ground, but saw nothing except a hind and a lovely white fawn. The pretty creatures fed close to me whilst sitting under the lee of a rock having some luncheon; and I watched them with much interest as they gambolled about, quite unconscious of danger, within forty yards of me. Reuben suggested that the fawn's skin would make a good rug; and so it would have, and a very handsome one, but nothing would induce me to molest them. The Baronet remained in camp, but saw nothing. It now became evident to us that our camp, though favourably chosen for passing deer, and selected by the Indians with that view, was badly placed for stalking, as we had to walk for miles to get to dry barrens; we therefore decided to shift our ground to some high barrens to the south and west of us.

The following day the Baronet, with one Indian, proceeded in the former direction, whilst Baird and I, with Reuben, went in the other, leaving our heavy gear in the camp in charge of the blue-jackets. My Irish setter, "Paddy," came with us, as we thought we might shoot some grouse on our way, but, unfortunately, he lost us a fine stag which we came suddenly upon. The deer was standing looking at us not more than a hundred yards off, but seeing the dog, which he probably took for a wolf, turned tail and bolted before we could get our rifles ready. We also met some wild geese, but failed to get a shot at them. Rather disgusted with our bad luck we reached an old "tilt" about noon, and deposited our gear therein. This tilt had been used by sportsmen before, and though in a dilapidated condition, proved most acceptable; a few boughs made it wind-tight, and the smoke going up through a hole in the roof kept the snow from coming down.

In the afternoon we went off to try some new and likely-looking barrens. A heavy north-west gale was blowing, with squalls of snow, and it was hard work to keep ourselves warm. After walking some miles we ascended a peak called the "Indians' Look-out," from the top of which we had a splendid view of the country. Far below us a lovely valley was spread out, scattered with woods and lakes, and looking in the distance like a park; beyond this a chain of mountains extended to the sea, which we could discern some thirty or forty miles off.

Reuben told us that from the top of this height the Indians spied the deer, and easily killed them as they ascended the pass immediately below the look-out: in fact, a more perfect place for a deer-drive could not be imagined. The bitter cold wind prevented us from fully enjoying the beautiful scene before us, and we gladly descended and took shelter in some woods at the back, where we made a small fire to thaw our boots and stockings. Refreshed by a soothing pipe we proceeded cautiously along, looking out for deer, when Reuben exclaimed, "Look, captain, big stag!" as a gleam of sunshine lit upon the snow-white[1] neck of a noble beast. The deer was trotting along, evidently on the track of others; we ran to cut him off, but he disappeared into the wood, so there was nothing for it but to follow. Reuben now led the way, eyes on the ground, noting every blade of grass pressed, stone turned, or mud stirred, and going at a run the whole time. The trail would have been easy enough to follow but for the numerous tracks all leading the same way, showing that a large company of deer had preceded us to the valley below. We now struck down through a thick wood, picking our way by the leads or open passes, well trodden by deer, when, through a space in the trees, I happened to catch a glimpse of some white objects in the valley. A glance through the glasses made them out to be deer, and the big stag's hurry to get into that valley became apparent. Picking our way cautiously along we presently reached the valley, and found ourselves within a few hundred yards of the deer. They were scattered about

---

[1] The big stags are almost white in October, their necks entirely so.

feeding amongst some immense boulders and small firs, and we had no difficulty in getting to within 150 yards of the nearest hind, but no stag could we see.

A heavy squall now came on, with blinding snow, and we waited for it to clear. Suddenly we saw a splendid stag come out of the wood behind us, accompanied by a hind, evidently the same old fellow we had seen before; but we had reached the valley by a short cut, whilst he had followed the track of the others, and had picked up a mistress by the way, and was in search of more. The two beasts looked like ghosts coming so silently through the blinding snow. Reuben now climbed upon a rock, and, much to our delight, said he saw two fine stags—one in charge of the party, the other we had just seen. A great commotion now became evident amongst the hinds, and presently we saw their lord and master galloping about in a state of excitement, calling in the stragglers, prodding them with his horns lest any should escape, and generally preparing for battle. It was precisely the same tactics as would be performed by a man-of-war convoying a fleet of merchantmen when an enemy appeared.

During this time we crept up to get a shot, but the stag was not still for a moment. Once I got him and a hind in a line, and might have killed them both with a single ball; but I didn't want the hind, and the snow was coming down so heavily it was difficult to see the sights of the rifle, so I let the opportunity pass, and was very glad I did so. Reuben now tried to "tole" the stag, but he took no notice of the ruse, well knowing that his real antagonist, whom he must have winded by this time, was coming down to rob him of his harem. Immediately we heard the challenge of the other stag to windward; and he had not long to wait, for the master of the herd started off at a gallop, and disappeared from our view. A moment later, and a crash as of a tree falling resounded through the valley, as the two stags' heads met in the arena.

Now was our time: taking no further notice of the hinds, we ran for the spot. The hinds ran also—not away from us, but with us; and the extraordinary sight might have been seen of three men and some sixteen or seventeen hinds all mixed up together to witness as pretty a fight as ever man beheld. In my experience of deer-stalking, extending over many years, I never saw the like or expect to see again—the scene was so grand and wild, very different from half-tame deer fighting in a park, or even in the Highlands, where they are not unaccustomed to the sight of man. There, amidst the blinding snow, were the two monarchs of the glen, their heads down, backs arched, horns crashing, turf flying, struggling, writhing, and pushing for the mastery. The hinds, for whom the battle was raging, assembled themselves round to see fair-play; and we stood and watched the combat from ten yards' distance. The combatants were well matched as regards size and weight, but the new arrival was the fresher of the two, and had longer horns. The owner of the seraglio had also a lovely head, with massive symmetrical horns; but, exhausted by the cares and anxiety attendant on his large family, he was slowly and surely giving way, when we decided to put an end to the contest. Selecting the nearest beast, I fired right and

STAGS FIGHTING

left into his squirming body, and Baird simultaneously did the same with the other. The stags, who had paid no sort of attention to us, now separated. One reeled and made an effort to charge, but rolled over as a third ball pierced his carcass; the other made off, but had not gone far before two more shots, fired at the same instant, dropped him also, and the two gladiators lay dead within a couple of hundred yards of each other.

The whole scene was a fit subject for an artist's pencil, and I wish that I could do justice to it; the wild beauty of the place and the heavy snowstorm raging at the time adding much to the effect. A few moments later and the scene had changed from one of intense excitement and full of life to perfect calm; the squall passed, the sun shone brightly, the stags lay dead, with faces upturned to the cloudless sky, and the hinds had departed.

We sat down to rest and smoke a pipe, while Reuben performed the last rites. Our two stags were noble specimens: I took the measurement of one of them according to

Whitaker's scale (see almanac) for measuring beasts. Thus, this stag measured 5 feet 2 inches in length from fore part of shoulder-blade along the back to root of tail, and 4 feet 10 inches in girth close behind the shoulder. The square of the girth in feet multiplied by five times the length, and the product divided by 21, shows a result of over 28 stone, which will be probably near the mark. This weight, 400 lb. nearly, represents the beast clean—*i.e.*, less head, horns, hoofs, offal, &c.—or the real market value of the meat. It must be considered, also, that these stags were greatly out of condition, without an ounce of fat on them, and that a month earlier they would have weighed certainly 100 lb. more. The above may be said to represent a fair "warrantable" stag in Newfoundland.

The day after this occurrence we sent Reuben back to our first camp to get assistance to bring in the heads, arranging to meet him in the valley in the afternoon. After being snowed up for several hours, Baird and I went out to get some grouse. We found a brood, and made a fine example of them, bagging eight, and then made our way into the valley, where our stags were lying. The remains were untouched, proving what I have always maintained, that wolves are not numerous in the island. We waited some time, and made a fire, but no Reuben appeared; so we started for home, but darkness overtook us before arriving at the wood where our tilt was, and we lost our way.[1] One belt of wood looked precisely like another in the dark, and we tramped backwards and forwards, knowing ourselves to be within a quarter of a mile of our camp, but unable to get there. We had almost resigned ourselves to a night on the barrens, wet through— no food, liquor, or matches, and no axe to cut firewood—thermometer below zero,—when providentially we noticed a blaze on a tree, and soon afterwards hit the trail; and most thankful were we to find ourselves once more in our snug tilt.[2] Reuben joined us next morning,

[1] There is a mocking-bird in Newfoundland whose cry, by a slight effort of imagination, may be thus interpreted: "Kennedy! Kennedy! Kennedy! Poor—lost Kennedy!" repeated at regular intervals. Our feelings on the subject may be better imagined than described.

[2] A small wigwam built of poles and bark—wind and water tight.

accounting for his absence by having met with and killed a stag on his way to camp.

Baird with my coxwain and the lumbermen now returned to the first camp, leaving me to go stalking with Reuben. We joined the others in the evening, not having seen anything except what looked like deer a long way off.

The Baronet also came back, having killed a pricket, much disgusted with his bad luck.

The next day all hands went to bring in meat, whilst Reuben and I took a stroll round, going first to his stag, which we decapitated and skinned; and taking his marrow-bones and some slices off the saddle for our luncheon, we went on to the tilt, five miles further on, where we made an excellent luncheon. Reuben roasted the venison on a stick, and cooked the marrow-bones in the embers; he also made some excellent bread in the wood-ashes. I never tasted anything better than meat cooked in this way. The Indian ate about 4 lb. of meat, filling his mouth and cutting the balance off square with his nose. We saw no more deer, so bagging a brace of grouse, returned to camp, preparatory to making an early start the next morning.

Whilst having our morning bath in a little stream that ran past our camp, one of the Indians reported three deer crossing the marsh. I had already completed my toilet; so seizing the rifle, I ran to cut them off, followed by the Baronet and Baird.

The former had nothing on but a shirt, a huge pair of boots, and a pair of spectacles, presenting a most ludicrous appearance. Baird, having no time to dress, had hastily donned a flushing ulster with a hood, in which original costume we ran across the marsh. The deer were approaching a small clump of wood in the centre of the marsh. Getting this in a line with them, I was able to get within shot; and perceiving an immense stag through the trees, I put a bullet into him. The stag was accompanied by a hind and calf: all three turned and galloped off; but the Baronet now opened fire, and with a brilliant shot tumbled the hind over at fully 250 yards. The sudden disappearance of his consort made the stag hesitate, and enabled me by running to cut him off. I found him standing in the middle of the marsh, looking very sick, whereupon I gave him both barrels from the rifle, and tumbled him headforemost into a bush. This stag was the biggest I ever killed, and I regret I did not measure him; but we were very much hurried, as I had to get down to the ship that day. His head was a good one, but nothing extra; but his foot was of enormous size. We measured this foot by the side of a bullock's on board the ship. They were about the same—the deer's, if anything, the larger. We brought his head and skin into camp, leaving the meat to be brought afterwards: the Indians said they got ten cents per lb. for meat, and nothing would be wasted.

Another stag presently appeared, and Baird tried to cut him off, but was unsuccessful.

I now started off with the Indians to get the boats ready for the rest of the party: and after a pretty hard day's work, reached the salt water at 8 P.M. The Baronet, not being very well satisfied with his luck, left us here to cross the island from east to west, which he succeeded in doing, but came very near being frozen in on the journey.

On our return to St John's in the Druid, my attention was called to a letter which had appeared in a New York paper, to the effect that Sir Rose Price and myself had massacred some thirty caribou, and that the Druid's rigging was adorned with trophies of the chase. The latter portion was substantially true; to the former I took exception in the following letter, which was printed in the 'New York Herald':—

"SIR,—I have observed with astonishment that, according to local papers, Sir Rose Price and I have slaughtered thirty caribou in Newfoundland quite lately. This statement is such a gross exaggeration, I shall be obliged to you to contradict it.

"If Sir R. Price and I had really been guilty of this butchery, we should be the last persons to boast of it, but as a matter of fact we did nothing of the kind. Sir R. Price killed four deer and I three, all good stags, and I do not think that too much after working hard for it, as we did. I have hunted in Newfoundland three years in succession, and always contented myself with three, or, at most, four stags. On each and all occasion I could have killed hinds by the dozen, but I can honestly say I never shot a hind in Newfoundland. I wish all sportsmen could say as much. As an old deer-stalker, I have naturally been annoyed at seeing my name in connection with wholesale slaughter, and I know that Sir Rose Price would be equally so. In justice, therefore, to us, I beg you to do me the favour to contradict the obnoxious article, and to convey to the author of it that he has been lying under a mistake. For my part, I would sooner be accused of manslaughter as of unsportsman-like behaviour.—I am, &c. W. R. K."

Paddy and Quashi.

CHAPTER XIII.

RANDOM NOTES ON SPORT.

I HAVE endeavoured in the preceding chapters to give an idea of the sport to be had on the barrens in the interior of Newfoundland; but even without attempting an expedition on so extensive a scale—which, of course, means time and money—very fair sport may be enjoyed in a quiet way with rod and gun in any part of the island. In fact, one could hardly make a mistake by camping out on the bank of any of the numerous rivers, or at the head of any of the fine harbours round the coast; such, for instance, as La Poile, White Bear Bay, Bay du Nord, Hare Bay, Long Harbour. Accommodation can occasionally be obtained in the telegraph office. The employees are always civil and most obliging; and the repairer having more time on his hands, is usually a good sportsman and a willing guide.

A party of us spent a couple of days and nights at the telegraph station at Long Harbour, and barring the mosquitoes, which were fearful, had a good time. There is a fine salmon-river within a stone's-throw of the house, and capital shooting on the barrens near at hand. We devoted one day to the wild geese. Accompanied by one of the officers, I started one morning after these wary birds, and we saw several flocks, but failed to get a shot for some time, owing to the vigilance of the sentry, who was always on the look-out. Our guide cleverly brought some towards us by imitating their cry and waving a handkerchief, but we failed to score, our shot being too light; however, we happened to mark down four on a loch, and by stalking them got within shot and bagged three of them. On our way back we saw quantities of grouse and some deer, but as it was the close season we did not molest them.

Our visit to Long Harbour came about in this way. Whilst at Havana we happened to fall in with the United States corvette Vandalia, commanded by Captain Richard Meade, an old friend of mine in the Pacific. At that time I commanded the Reindeer, and he a small American sloop. When next we met at Havana, Meade remarked, that whereas before I had the best ship, now he thought that he had, which was the case. Whilst discussing affairs in general, and the neglected condition of overworked, underpaid naval officers in particular, we agreed that if diplomatists would only allow us sailors to settle all matters of dispute where seafaring folk and nautical matters were concerned, how very much better it would be, alluding more especially to the Fortune Bay "outrage" in particular, which we flattered ourselves we could have settled in a day, and probably a few thousand dollars would have ended the matter.

I laughingly told Captain Meade to ask the Secretary for the United States Navy to send him up to Fortune Bay to meet me, and we would settle any further difficulties over our cigars and champagne. Whether he did so or not, I am unaware ; but I was somewhat amused, on receipt of a telegram from the Admiral, many months afterwards, ordering me to proceed to Fortune Bay to meet the Vandalia—on such and such a date. I was there punctually to time, but as the Vandalia was not, I devoted the spare time to shooting and fishing.

On my return from this wild-goose chase aforementioned, I was told the Vandalia had arrived; so, instead of going direct on board the Druid, I went straight to the Vandalia to see my old friend. It was a dark and stormy night, and the officer of the watch was not a little surprised to see a wet, dirty figure coming on board dragging a wild goose by the neck. The cabin-door sentry wanted to stop me, but I explained that I was the captain's cook of the Druid, and wished to see the captain; so was admitted, and we had a good time together. Next day I returned Captain Meade's official visit in cocked hat and epaulets.[1]

I have reason to remember Long Harbour, for it was there my best salmon-rod was lost, on this very night, I believe. It was a beautiful rod,

---

[1] The last time I saw the gallant captain he was perfecting an infernal machine for the destruction of the entire British navy!

built by Forrest, of Kelso, for a very dear friend, and given to me. It is supposed to have been lost overboard from the steam-cutter when coming alongside, which sad event was not communicated to me till next morning, when the ship was searched without success. The rod had been stowed away in its cover, and must have sunk. To try the experiment as to the floatation of a rod—of course without the reel, which would sink it at once—I lowered my other rod into the water with a line fast to it: it at first floated, but as the cover got wet it sank level with the surface. This was a lighter rod than the missing one, which was made of greenheart, a very close-grained wood.

A reward was at once offered; search-parties were organised, who searched every bit of coast for miles; signalmen were on the look-out, divers sent down, but all to no purpose; and it became evident the rod was gone. A gloom was thrown over the whole ship's company when it was known that the captain's pet rod was lost. The skipper betook himself to his cabin, and was reported to be like a bear with a sore head, refusing to be comforted.

He had left orders not to be disturbed; no noise was permitted over his head; the sentry made his reports in a stealthy manner; and even his old and trusty friend the first lieutenant appeared with a saddened countenance when he joined the captain in his usual post-prandial cheroot. As for the faithful Norris, my coxwain, he durst not show himself for three days, and then, with tears in his eyes, admitted that he feared "we should never—never—see—that lovely—rod—again." At last, to prevent the entire demoralisation of the ship's company, the doctor recommended complete change of air and scene, so we sadly steamed away.

Our destination was Storey Harbour, also in Fortune Bay, which place had never been visited by a man-of-war since the days of Captain Cook, and I have reason to believe that that gallant navigator never entered it. The only chart of the place was one of Cook's; but as his are as a rule wonderfully accurate, considering the time and means at his disposal in those days, we steamed up the long tortuous channel leading to the harbour with perfect confidence.

It was a lovely day, and all hands were on deck as we neared the entrance, when, just as we opened the harbour, we ran crash upon a rock in mid-channel, and bounded over it into deep water. As soon as the anchor was dropped, we sounded the well, and sent divers down to examine the bottom. They reported that a great piece of keel was wanting, so we were ordered forthwith to Halifax for repairs; and thus the episode of the rod was forgotten.

On sounding about the rock, we found only two feet on it at dead low water. It was not marked on the chart, but was well known to the local fishermen. One old man told us he had fished about that rock all his life, and, said he, "When I seed the frigate a-coming in, I says to my boy, she's on the rock surely; and so you be."

Another good all-round sporting place is Hare Bay, on the south coast. A very pretty salmon-river discharges itself into the head of the bay; there are plenty of grouse on the barrens, and we also invariably saw bears there: the place is uninhabited.

On one occasion the ship's steward came

face to face with two bears, so he promptly bolted, and never ceased running till he reached the beach. We made up a party and went after those bears, but never found them, although we saw where they had been, and the place smelt like the bear-house at the Zoological Gardens.

At White Bear Bay (so called because a polar bear has never been heard of in that locality), the telegraph-repairer had a narrow escape from a black bear. He told me that he set a spring-gun for one in the vicinity of the bears' cave; and one evening he heard a report, so he went to see the result. The bear had evidently been wounded, and had made good its escape to a cave; so the next morning the man, accompanied by his dog, went in search of him. On reaching the cave the bear charged out, and, taking no notice of the dog, went straight for the man. The first barrel missed fire, and the poor fellow was so agitated that he tugged at the trigger of the second barrel till he broke it; but the gun went off and killed the bear, which was then close upon him. He had got the skin, which was a very fine one.

Two of our middies, whilst out shooting at this place, got lost, and being overtaken by the darkness, and fearing to fall over a precipice, had to remain on the hills all night without fire or food. We were very anxious concerning them, and landed a relief-party, headed by the first lieutenant, with guns, rockets, and blue-lights, but they failed to find them. The lads turned up next morning, none the worse for their adventure.

Talking of bears reminds me of a ridiculous affair that happened in Lark Harbour in the Bay of Islands. I had gone ashore to look for geese, accompanied as usual by my coxwain, a big burly fellow, who, according to the habit of blue-jackets, took off his boots and walked barefooted. We followed the shore for some miles, leaving a trail upon the sand. Some of our officers also landed, and struck my trail, followed, as they supposed, by a bear.

It is a well-known fact that a bear's trail closely resembles that of a man, and may be easily mistaken for it. It seemed evident that the unfortunate skipper was being tracked by the ferocious and bloodthirsty animal, and the officers gallantly gave chase, in hopes of slaying the bear before he had made a meal of the captain. After following the track for some time, it became apparent that the skipper and the bear had sat down and made a friendly meal together, so the officers returned on board, and I am afraid got well chaffed for their trouble.

The neighbourhood of Colinet, not far from St John's, is a favourite resort for sportsmen. A young relative of mine was shooting there, and had had very poor luck, when the dogs began drawing, and then came to a steady point. Here at last are the birds, he thought; but as nothing got up, he walked forward, only to find a huge flat-fish, alive and kicking! and this was three miles from the salt water. The fish must have been dropped by an osprey, which had probably been disturbed before it could make a meal of it.

There is another Hare Bay on the north-east coast of Newfoundland, which is a good sporting locality. Thousands of wild ducks breed at this place, and there are two fine rivers in it, both holding salmon and sea-trout. The south river used to be barred, and fished by a Frenchman, and was therefore ruined for rod-fishing; but in the other I killed as many trout up to 3 lb. as we could carry. We saw a very remarkable mirage in this fine bay. There are several islands dotted about, and on this occasion a few small icebergs: on looking to seaward, we saw the whole of the islands and icebergs reflected in the sky, but upside-down, the visionary ones just touching the tops of the real ones. I made a sketch of this curious scene. Whilst fishing in the south-west brook, my setter Paddy disturbed a couple of snipe which had their nest hard by. I called him off, when the parent birds, after twittering round at my feet, both flew up to the very top of a high tree, where they perched. I have heard of this before, but never saw it but on that occasion.

Another yarn and I have done, else the reader will think I am romancing. One day I was crossing a river in a canoe with an Indian, and as the craft touched the shore, a large bittern rose from the reeds which fringed the banks. Reuben—for it was he—quickly slipped his axe from his belt, where Indians always keep it, and cut the bird down in the air, merely remarking as he did so, "He do for salmon-fly."

I must not omit to mention in the list of sporting places the fine harbour of La Poile, where we often anchored. There is a settlement near the entrance of the harbour, but the mouth of the river is ten miles further up. By following the main branch of the stream another five miles of most villanous walking, a first-rate camping-place will be found, close to what they call the salmon-hole. This is simply a deep pool confined by rocky banks on either side, a most romantic and secluded spot, where a party of sportsmen could pitch their camp without fear of molestation, for there is not a living soul nearer than the settlement, fifteen miles off. The river abounds with salmon and sea-trout; the barrens are well stocked with grouse, and are easy of access; and there are plenty of deer within a day's march, or say fifteen miles from the valley. Supplies of all kinds can be got at the settlement, and the storekeeper is, or used to be, a very obliging man. La Poile has also the advantage of being a port of call for the coastal steamers, so it is easy to get at.

Altogether, I do not know any place combining so many advantages. There is another spot I have in my mind's eye, but little known, and seldom visited, and then only by a man-of-war, called Little River. The entrance is so narrow that it is scarcely visible from seaward, being a mere cleft in the rocks, which rise almost perpendicularly on either side; a narrow but steep channel, clear of all dangers, leads to a magnificent basin. To any one possessing a steam-yacht, I can recommend this beautiful harbour. The settlement is four miles from the entrance; we visited it twice in the Druid, firing our guns for the echo; and at night we illuminated the ship, for the edification of the unsophisticated inhabitants.

A very snug anchorage is Port au Basque—commonly called Channel; and although there is no river flowing into the harbour, a beautiful stream flows into the neighbouring bay, called Grand Bay Brook. This can be reached either by walking over the barrens or by dragging a boat over a neck of land, and launching it on the other side, when the river can be at once entered. A long "steady" of deep still water terminates in a series of tumbling cascades, with lovely pools for salmon; above this again is a series of rapids and pools for four or five miles, ending, as most of the rivers in Newfoundland do, in a magnificent deep pool with precipitous banks, and a splendid fall at the head, flowing out of the lake, from whence the river takes its rise. I noticed about the fall several circular holes in the rocks, deeply scored, with perfect regularity and smoothness; and I could not make out what had caused these holes, which are quite different from the grooves made by ice, as may be seen on all the rocks in that country. At last I discovered the cause, quite accidentally; in one of the holes was a stone, which revolved round with the eddying waters. This stone had probably lodged in a depression, and by the action of the water for ages past had made the hole, and worn itself round in doing so. I have since seen the same in Scotland, wherever there is a heavy fall of water; and under the bridge at Killin, in Perthshire, one may be seen, which I measured, four feet deep. But in some cases there is no stone at the bottom of the hole. How it could get out I cannot say, especially in an uninhabited spot, where no one would remove it; perhaps it may have worn itself out.

I fished Grand Bay Brook one day from its source to the sea; took out twelve trout, weighing 36 lb., and on another occasion a small grilse. There are salmon in it; but I fear it is very much poached.

But I might multiply these sort of sporting paradises *ad infinitum*, as my mind carries me back to the old familiar scenes. Some of the best of them are inaccessible to the casual traveller, and can only be visited by a man-of-war. If I were asked which is the best river in Newfoundland or Labrador, I should say the East river, at Hawke's Bay, for the former, and Forteau river for the latter. In both these rivers a fine salmon-pool will be met with, not far from the mouth; and at each pool a large rock will be seen near the head, upon which many naval captains have stood, rod in hand. Should any one have the luck to be at Hawke's Bay, on or about the 12th July, or at Forteau about the 20th, I will guarantee him fine sport. It is a curious fact that the salmon enter the rivers almost to a day,—and a remarkable coincidence that H.M. ships are generally to be found at those spots about the same time! It is fortunate that duty and pleasure may often be combined. Bonne Bay, on the west coast, has also some noble streams; and Deer Brook, one of the smallest of them, cannot be beat for sea-trout.

Some idea of the extent of the Labrador fishery may be gathered from the fact that upwards of a thousand fishing-vessels visit that coast annually, carrying between 30,000 and 40,000 men, mostly from Newfoundland. The season opens about the middle of June, and lasts till October. Many of the fishery-fleet carry women, to aid in curing the fish. It is impossible to overrate the importance of these fisheries, and it is calculated that one-third of the whole catch of cod-fish is taken on the Labrador coast. There are at least 1000 miles of coast available for fishing purposes, and Professor Hind estimates the total area of this vast fishing-ground at upwards of 7000 square miles. On the whole of this, cod, herrings, salmon, mackerel, and lobsters abound; in fact, the fisheries of the Labrador may be said to be inexhaustible. The seal-fishery is a very lucrative and important industry. Quite a fleet of steamers, carrying from 200 to 300 men each, is employed in it, and the average capture of seals is estimated at 300,000 to 400,000 in a single season.

But with regard to Labrador, my information must necessarily be somewhat meagre, seeing that our visits there were few and far between, and then were generally restricted to the south coast; so that with the exception of the Forteau river, one of the best, I really am no authority.

But I feel confident that some grand sport is to be obtained in that country by any one who is prepared to rough it. There are many fine rivers in the Newfoundland division of Labrador, such as the Eagle river, second to none in the Canadian portion; and I have little doubt that as good sport could be obtained there as on the Mingan river, or other famous streams of Canada or New Brunswick.

Caribou are said to be very plentiful in Labrador, but I cannot speak from experience. Grouse and curlew are found in abundance, besides other game.

The country is bleak and sparsely populated, and but little is known of it, except perhaps to the missionaries who reside there, and the clergy who periodically visit it. Even our good Bishop of Newfoundland has to brave the stormy ocean in a 30-ton yawl to make his yearly visit to those barren shores.[1] Certainly the clergy in those regions have no sinecure; and a man must not only have his heart in his work, but be also a good sailor and able to rough it to do his duty. All honour to such noble men; their motto is, Deeds, not words.

I have now, I think, touched on most subjects which are likely to interest the reader, and it only remains for me to bid adieu to Newfoundland, with its iron-bound coasts, its fogs, and ice. But notwithstanding these slight drawbacks, I confess to a warm regard for the dear old colony; for do I not know that within that icy barrier there are warm hearts and true hos-

[1] Bermuda is also included in his diocese.

pitality! For three successive seasons I had circumnavigated those shores, made acquaintance with some of its rocks, inhaled the fogs, and had friendly rubs against the ice, in all of which encounters the poor old Druid got the worst of it, bearing scars upon her hull which she will carry to her grave.

At last the day arrived when we took our departure, and turned our faces to the sunny south, to meet with fresh adventures in a different clime. But never shall I forget the many happy days I have passed in that grand old island; and as the Druid sped swiftly on her way towards Halifax, with her canvas swelling to the breeze and the water foaming at her bows, I took a last lingering look over her counter, wondering if I should ever see those shores again.

It is gratifying to me to find that, since these lines were penned, my hopes regarding the colony have been to a great extent realised.

The railway which is to connect the capital with the mining regions, touching the principal towns, and opening up the most fertile lands

R

for settlement, has been commenced, and already several miles of it are in working order, and its completion is, I believe, expected shortly. That this will confer an inestimable benefit on the colony, cannot be doubted.

Not less in importance is the prospect of the so called "French Shore" question being virtually settled, by the local Government being empowered to issue grants of land for mining and agricultural purposes. A rapid increase of the population on those shores may therefore be expected.

The appointment of magistrates on that part of the coast is also an important fact, which should give contentment to the fishermen of Newfoundland, while the claims of the French will also be respected.

These measures will go far to promote that harmony between the two countries which has been wanting in the past, but which is so much to be desired.

CHAPTER XIV.

BERMUDA, WEST INDIES, AND THE SPANISH MAIN.

AFTER a short spell at Halifax, that paradise of naval officers, we proceeded regularly every season to Bermuda, to refit and prepare for the West Indies, where we spent three successive winters, arriving at Port Royal, Jamaica, in time to eat our Christmas dinner, and leaving the West Indies again on our northern passage about the end of March or early in April, so as to reach St John's on or before the Queen's birthday. In this way we visited Bermuda on our annual migrations north and south no less than seven times, during the commission of three and a half years. A passing glance at these lovely islands may, therefore, be not out of place here.

Moore's "beautiful isle of the sea." Opinions are divided as to whether Bermuda is an earthly paradise or one of the most monotonous places under heaven. Bermudians declare the former to be the case; most naval officers, and probably military ones also, incline to the latter opinion: the truth lies between the two.

The approach to the islands from seaward is certainly very lovely, and the pleasing impression remains after one has skirted the reefs at the entrance and come to an anchor inside. The first thing that attracts the eye of a new-comer is the wonderful clearness and lovely colouring of the water, a pale greenish blue, and the beautiful whiteness of the coral strand. The water is so clear that the reefs are plainly visible, and it would be possible for even a stranger to thread his way between them on a clear day. But ships are obliged to take a pilot, and indeed it would be safer to do so in any case, as the channels are narrow, and a mistake with the helm will at once put a ship ashore; besides, with the sun in one's eyes, the reefs and buoys are not easily seen. The contrast between the snowy white houses and the dark foliage of the juniper-cedar is especially beautiful and refreshing to the eye, wearied by the monotony of gazing on the sea for several days previously. It would be difficult to find a more lovely spot than Admiralty House, the residence of the Commander-in-Chief for several months in the winter; or Mount Langton, the Governor's permanent residence. The senior naval officer's house on Ireland Island is also an enchanting spot, built in the bungalow style, with a broad verandah round, and enveloped in a wealth of foliage. Curiously enough, the two most beautiful places on that side are the hospital and the cemetery! The reason why there is so much diversity of opinion regarding Bermuda is because naval officers are destined to see the worst part of it. The ships are usually moored alongside the camber, where the dockyard is, for convenience in refitting; a hot, dusty, glaring place, swarming with flies and mosquitoes, and from which there is but one way of escape, a dreary, monotonous, dusty road.

For those fond of yachting and boat-sailing, or sea-fishing, Bermuda presents unusual attractions. The sky is of the bluest; the water a lovely emerald-green, revealing in its depths wonderful corals, sponges, shells, and sea-weeds, with many kinds of brilliantly marked fish swimming about their rocky home. Overhead the snow-white "boatswain" birds circle round, the delicate tints of the water being reflected on their breasts.

For several months in the year the climate is most agreeable — a fresh sea-breeze blows through the day; and a more enjoyable expedition can hardly be imagined than a trip over to Hamilton, the caves of Walshingham, or Harrington Sound, in one of the celebrated 'Mudian boats. These boats are unequalled in their own waters at beating to windward, but their model is defective. They are no good off the wind, as they would soon run themselves under water, and, being heavily ballasted, would go down like a stone. Moreover, in a sea-way they would pitch their mast over the bows, and from their bluff entrance would not hold their own against any of our crack yachts, of their own tonnage, either on or off the wind. They are, however, most picturesque and handy, and are well suited for the waters for which they are intended.

In Harrington Sound there is a place called the Devil's Hole, where sea-fish are kept to fatten. This hole or cave is open at the top, and being connected with the sea by subterraneous passages, the tide ebbs and flows into it, thus keeping it always sweet. The fish are caught outside on the reefs and placed in here till required: they are fed regularly, and get very fat and saucy, coming over to the side and grabbing at anything offered them, even a pocket-handkerchief. The hole is very deep, so the fish do not lose their eyesight, as deep-sea fishes will when put into shallow water. Some of these monsters weigh thirty and forty pounds, and are very voracious. I once drew a spoon-bait across the hole; it was chased by the whole lot: one seized it, and I had a great job to get him out, as he dived deep and got under a ledge. Sharks and turtle are occasionally put into this place: the angel-fish are especially pretty and graceful.

For deep-sea fishing the natives use a water-telescope, which is merely a long square box with a glass at one end. By lowering this apparatus into the water, everything becomes visible as though there was no water: the effect is quite beautiful, as the fish can be seen swimming about amongst the lovely corals, shells, and sea-weed which clothe the bottom of these seas.

Hamilton, the capital of the islands, is beautifully situated at the head of a fine bay, surrounded on all sides by well-wooded hills. In this neighbourhood are many fine country-houses, belonging to the well-to-do merchants, snugly nestling amongst lovely gardens, their white walls often nearly hidden by roses, geraniums, and many kinds of flowers, azaleas being especially common. Even the residences of the humbler classes are models of neatness and comfort; in this respect Bermuda will bear favourable comparison with any part of the world. It is the cleanest little place I ever saw, the houses so tidy, the roads so well kept, —nowhere is there any evidence of squalor or poverty. The people may be poor, but they all look contented and happy in that bright sunny clime. As there are no fresh-water lakes, or rivers, the rain-water is collected in huge tanks, and the supply is always equal to the demand. The soil on the principal islands is very rich, and the finest crops of potatoes, tomatoes, and onions are raised, and shipped in large quantities to the United States. There are no birds indigenous to the islands that I am aware of, but birds of passage frequently visit it, either from choice or blown off from the mainland. In this way ducks and snipe are occasionally heard of in the marshes, when the whole garrison turns out. The Virginian quail have been introduced and multiplied, also the Virginian cardinal, and a very pretty blue bird about the size of a sparrow : these two last add greatly to the quiet beauty of the woods by their brilliant colouring. They are, I believe, now protected by law.

Life at these islands must necessarily be somewhat monotonous. No telegrams disturb the serenity of the inhabitants, and for upwards of twenty years that I have known the place, I have observed but little change. Many prefer it as it is; but it is certainly monstrous that a military and naval station of such importance should not be in telegraphic communication with Halifax, the West Indies, and the United States. Geographically speaking, Bermuda is admirably situated, being a half-way port for our ships going to and from the northern to the southern part of the station. As a fortress it is impregnable, being guarded on every side by a natural reef, extending for miles in almost all directions. The passages through these reefs are known only to the local pilots, who are sworn to secrecy; and by taking up the buoys and substituting torpedoes, it would be very awkward for any enemy's ship to approach. Even if she once got inside, she ought never to get out again. At any rate, as the Yankee said when his cow was run over by an express train, she would probably be " somewhat discouraged." Americans have taken to visiting the islands of late years, and have infused a good deal of energy into the community. A hotel has sprung up, and fast steamers now run the mails to and from New York, making the passage in a little over fifty hours. At certain seasons of the year violent gales sweep over the islands, and in fact they may be said to lie directly in the path of the West India hurricanes. During the summer the heat is most oppressive, oily calms prevail for days together, and the mosquitoes and flies render one's life a burden. To sum up Bermuda in a few words, it is a pleasant place to spend a few weeks in the winter-time; but as a permanent residence, I would not care about it!

There are several routes from Bermuda to the West Indies—the Windward, the Crooked Island, and the Mona passage. For a sailing-ship the last is perhaps the safest, and it was this route we generally selected in the Druid, so as to carry fair winds, and thus enable us to make the passage as much as possible under sail, and also avoid the dangerous shoals which infest the more direct steamer's route.

Nine or ten days' pleasant sailing usually carried us to Port Royal, the headquarters of H.M. ships on the Jamaica division of the West Indies. The first appearance of the island of Jamaica is exceedingly beautiful, especially if approaching from the eastward. The blue mountains rise to upwards of 5000 feet, and are clothed almost to their summits with tropical vegetation. As one approaches nearer, the valleys may be observed to be well cultivated with sugar, tobacco, Indian corn, interspersed with cocoa-nut and banana plantations. Drawing nearer to Kingston, the capital of the island, the country assumes a more arid appearance, and has justly been likened to a piece of brown paper crumpled up, until at last the acme of desolation is reached at Port Royal, where the dockyard is situated, and where moorings are laid down for H.M. ships. Merchant vessels proceed to Kingston, four or five miles further, at the head of a fine bay.

The usual custom for H.M. ships stationed at Jamaica, under the orders of the Commodore, is to remain only a short time at Port Royal, and then, after visiting the harbours on the north side of the island, to give leave to the men, proceed on a cruise to Cuba, Haïti, Belize, or the Spanish Main. I propose, after a few remarks on Jamaica itself, to relate our experience of the others as we visited them. I have every reason to speak kindly of this island—three successive winters having been passed most pleasantly in the West Indies, with our headquarters at Jamaica,—mostly at Port Royal, it is true, but also visiting the beautiful harbours on the northern shores; so that, like most naval officers, I have been able to form a pretty good idea of the island. Jamaica has, I fear, a bad name at home—a name too often associated with earthquakes, hurricanes, and yellow-jack; but in reality, the last place one hears of such things is at Jamaica itself. I am sure that statistics would show that Jamaica was as healthy a place as there is on the globe, and far more so than Malta or Gibraltar, Cyprus or Halifax. At all these places, fevers, smallpox, diphtheria, or bronchitis, are common enough; whereas at Jamaica they are rare. Fever of a remittent type is not uncommon amongst Europeans, caused generally by undue exertion or exposure to the sun; but this is only a question of quinine, and is not often serious. As to yellow fever, it is almost unknown, unless brought there from Havana, Haïti, or Colon. As a matter of fact, there was not one single case of yellow fever at Port Royal during the whole time we were there—three winters, off and on; and for a whole year there was not one death in the Naval Hospital from any cause whatever! What place could say the same? As for earthquakes, there was a very bad one in 1692, which swallowed up Port Royal—since when, there has not been anything to speak of. As regards hurricanes, there was a bad one three or four years ago, which did a deal of damage; but there had not been one for sixty years previously. These facts speak for themselves. The fact is, the climate is good enough for those who take ordinary precautions, and are moderate in eating and drinking. Many people are able to live out there in health and comfort who would die in England. During the summer months the heat is unpleasant, but seldom oppressive, except, perhaps, on the low grounds; but the climate of the hills is always delightful, and speedily restores the bloom to the cheeks of ladies and children who have found their constitutions tried by the hot weather. Like all these Leeward West India islands, the north side is far superior to the south: the temperature is far more genial, and the scenery more beautiful; rains are more abundant, and the foliage more luxuriant. A more lovely spot can hardly be imagined than Ocho Rios, with its wonderful ferns and orchids, and its tumbling cascades. Port Antonio is also a beautiful spot, so is Lucea, and Montego Bay. All these places are on the north side, exposed to the pure and healthy sea-breeze from the Atlantic.

From my own experience, I can honestly aver that the hospitality for which Jamaica has always been justly celebrated has not died out, although I fear in many cases the planters are not in the position to entertain as they once were. Still, be they rich or poor, I am bound to say that we were always heartily welcomed wherever we went; and what more could we desire?

As regards the planters, I fear their look-out is not a bright one, and I suspect that the sugar estates which are paying a dividend could be counted on one's fingers. How can it be otherwise, when labour is so difficult to procure? It is the fashion to abuse the black man for a lazy rascal, who won't work. Well, perhaps he is; but I should like to know who would work, if he had all he wanted in the matter of food and clothing without having to work for it? Certainly not the labouring classes in England, nor any other country. They work simply because they would starve if they didn't. The black man in Jamaica can't starve, and he works just sufficiently to keep himself and his family alive, which means a couple of days a-week. A few bananas keep him going; and a little patch of ground to grow cassava, yams, sugar-cane, or cocoa, which require little cultivation, is enough for his wants. The women carry the produce into market, obtaining the wherewithal to pay the rent and taxes (a few shillings per annum), and keep them in clothing, which is not a very heavy item in a tropical climate, where the grown-up people wear but little, and the children nothing at all.

The importation of coolie labour has been tried, and I believe successfully, on some estates; but the coolie does not as a rule care to remain in the country. He saves every penny, and having piled his savings, in the shape of bangles and necklaces, on to the person of his wife and himself, embarks by the first coolie-ship, and returns to his native country. Probably Chinamen would do well. In all countries where Chinese labour has been introduced — witness California, Peru, &c.—they have undoubtedly been the means of developing the resources of the country, care being taken not to let the Chinamen increase and multiply too rapidly. In California this is regulated by stopping the flow of emigration, or shipping them back to their own country. In Peru a simpler and speedier method has been adopted—*i.e.*, wholesale massacre, which is doubtless a convenient method of ridding themselves of a troublesome intruder! The emancipation of the slaves has been the ruin of many fine estates in Jamaica. One has only to drive into the country in any direction to see the remains of what were once fine houses, and the ruins of sugar-factories, —truly a sad scene of desolation.

There are, however, other industries besides sugar to be considered, requiring less labour, and it is in this direction that prosperity will, I believe, eventually return to Jamaica. According to late statistics, I see that the value of the sugar and rum exported in the year 1882 would, it is estimated, reach one million sterling.

Coffee has declined in value owing to the low price of the article at home, but the exportation of logwood and pimento has increased. The cultivation of tobacco has been attempted on a large scale, and Jamaica cigars are now familiar in the London market. Our experience of them, however, would not give them the preference over genuine havanas. But the most important industry attempted of late years is the cultivation of cinchona,[1] which is being prosecuted with wonderful success by Mr Morris, the Government botanist, whose estate is picturesquely situated 5000 feet above the level of the sea. Mr Morris is doing a great deal to permanently benefit the island. Besides cinchona, he has, I understand, a quantity of young teak, mahogany, and cedar trees ready for distribution to those who care to have them.

Cattle-rearing is a risky business, except in some of the favoured parts of the island, where droughts are unknown. On the lowlands, where the rainfall is uncertain, irrigation becomes necessary, and this enters into expense. The raising of fat cattle has, moreover, been over-

[1] Quinine.

done, and the breed has in consequence depreciated in value.

The rainfall seems to be cut off by the mountainous range in the interior, and is very unequally divided. On the south side people are often starved for want of water, while on the north they have abundance—often too much. Naturally the whole features of the country are altered: the southern slopes of the mountains have a barren and withered appearance, and the plains are parched, hot, and dusty. The north side is precisely the reverse: here may be seen tropical vegetation in all its glory, with lovely flowers, ferns, and orchids to delight the naturalist. Most of the fruit is grown on this side, and immense quantities of bananas and cocoa-nuts are shipped to the United States —mostly from Port Antonio, a very flourishing and rising little place with an excellent harbour. For lovers of scenery, no more beautiful spot could be found than the Bog Walk or the public gardens at Castleton. The neighbourhood of Chapelton is also very beautiful; nowhere have I seen such magnificent clusters of bamboo as in this district.

The question of droughts is becoming a very serious consideration, and one may naturally inquire, how are they caused? They used not to exist in former years to the extent they do now. I am therefore driven to the conclusion that they must in a measure be caused by interference with the laws of nature. In all countries where timber has been wantonly cut down without replanting, drought succeeds. Madeira is an instance of this, so is Mauritius. The former, as its name implies (*madera* being Spanish for wood), was once thickly wooded; what is it now? The vines have been destroyed by drought, caused by cutting down the timber wholesale. Mauritius suffered severely by the destruction of forest-trees until it was stopped; and Jamaica is undergoing the same process—the heavy timber being ruthlessly destroyed at such a rate as to seriously affect the rainfall. According to Mr Espeut, there are upwards of eighty kinds of valuable trees in Jamaica—most of them of use for building ships, houses, carts, fences, shingling roofs, staves for casks, or suitable for masts and spars. Among the most useful of these are the teak, mahogany, cedar, box, pimento, mahoe, cashew, rosewood, lancewood, ebony, Spanish oak, naseberry, fustic, yacca, Santa Maria, &c. A very valuable wood named Tibrush is largely used by the Caribs of Honduras for making dug-outs — *i.e.*, canoes dug from a single tree. I do not think this wood is known in Jamaica. The negroes are in the habit of cutting down these fine trees indiscriminately for the purpose of cultivating the land. This would be all very well, provided that they kept it under permanent cultivation, which they do not. After a year or so they leave that clearing and move on, destroying more timber to get fresh soil. These clearings soon become jungle, and no fresh trees are planted. In this way thousands of acres of forest are destroyed. Unless Government put a stop to this practice, rains will cease to a great extent, and agriculture must suffer.

A great drawback to Jamaica (and I suppose the same applies to all our colonies more or less) seems to be the indifference with which so many regard the future of the country. Every one naturally hopes to go back to the "old country" some time or other, and the object seems to be to get all one can out of the island, and then clear out, leaving those who come after them to do the same. But there must be many residing in the colony who are destined to spend most of their days there, and can never hope to realise sufficient to live at home at ease. If such people would only face this fact, and reconcile themselves to it, they might, by devoting themselves to the permanent improvement of their estates, not only be more happy and contented themselves, but leave their families better provided for. Many people, I fancy, expect too much from a colony. They go out with a few thousands, and probably make a very fair living out of it for years, getting a good return for their investments, and living in fine style, with carriage and horses and servants; but because they don't make a fortune, think it "hard lines," and grumble at the place, forgetting that the same amount invested in England would have brought them only a small return, and far fewer comforts. One of the great nuisances the sugar-planters have had to contend against, has been the rats which swarmed over the island, destroying the canes, and killing poultry, &c. To get rid of these pests, the mongoos was introduced by Mr Espeut, and with such success that the rats have almost disappeared; and on sugar estates, where formerly they had to pay £200 and £300 per annum for killing rats, they now have to pay a mere trifle. But the mongoos has now multiplied to such a prodigious extent as to be nearly as great a nuisance as the rats. Already there are those who maintain that this little animal does more harm than good, by killing poultry; and probably he does, except to the sugar-planters. In the meantime, he may have credit for the good that he has done; what the verdict will be ten years hence, remains to be seen.

As regards the town of Kingston, there is not much to be said in its favour. In general appearance it bears no sort of comparison with either Havana or Matanzas, and in the matter of cleanliness it would hardly compare favourably with Port au Prince. There is not a single hotel in the town worthy the name—a couple of boarding-houses affording the only accommodation for passengers and visitors; consequently, any English tourists of position are entertained by the Governor at King's House,—a tax of no small consideration on his Excellency's hospitality. The harbour of Kingston is considered one of the best in the West Indies; but the sea-breeze, which often blows with great violence, sends in a considerable sea, making it frequently very dangerous for boats. The port might be improved by cutting through the palisadoes at the narrowest part, making the entrance to the eastward: by placing a lighthouse at this entrance, ships might enter the harbour at all times of night, and save a long detour.

Port Royal has been the bugbear of naval officers from time immemorial, and the bad name which it bears has been to a certain extent ascribed to Jamaica generally. But most unjustly so. As well might a person judge of England from a residence at Sheerness! In this respect I fear my own cloth are not guiltless, for I have known naval men abuse Jamaica who seldom left Port Royal, and never went further than Kingston. The place is bad enough, but, like many another place, is not half so bad as it is painted. The Commodore's house is a fine one, with a good billiard-table and plenty of baths—a great luxury in a hot climate; and the dockyard and hospital are models of cleanliness and good order. An officers' club and seamen's recreation rooms add greatly to the attractions of the place. The part called by courtesy the town is a

Port Royal, Jamaica.

collection of filthy hovels, but the authorities have no control over that. The whole place ought to be under the supervision of the Government: £20,000 would buy the ground, and the town might then be laid out with an eye to cleanliness and decency. Water might be brought down by pipes, laid along the palisadoes from the Hope river, or, if the fall be not sufficient, an iron steam-tank, capable of being also used as a tug, would answer the purpose, instead of the rotten old leaky wooden sailing-tanks which supply brackish water to the town and shipping as at present. Brackish water may be very wholesome, but, for my part, I never did hanker after it. When the cocoa-nut trees which have been planted round about the club and dockyard, &c., grow up, they will add much to the appearance of this much-abused place.

As regards sport in Jamaica, I have but little to say. Virginian quail are distributed all over the island, but are difficult to get at, as they fly into the dense bush at the first alarm. Wild guinea-fowl are also tolerably numerous. It is a curious fact that the wild birds have black legs and the tame ones yellow, showing that they are quite a different variety: I do not fancy they breed one with the other. Snipe and teal are to be found in the marshy lands, but my experience of shooting in Jamaica is, that the "game is not worth the candle." One cannot go into the bush without getting covered with ticks. These insects swarm in the grass, and cling to the person by hundreds. They are said to have been brought from Cuba with the cattle. It may be so; all I know is, I have shot in Cuba and never saw a tick. There are some very fine rivers in the island, useless for navigation, but full of fish, some of immense size and of good flavour. These rivers run down very rapidly in the dry season, and rise very fast in the wet, at times carrying all before them and rendering them most dangerous.

In some of the large rivers, such as the Cobre, the Rio Grande, Spanish River, Swift River, &c., there are fish of 20 lb. weight, and good sport may be had with spinning-tackle. They will occasionally take a fly, and I have hooked, but seldom landed them, owing to their sharp teeth cutting through the gut. It is good sport nevertheless, and very pleasant wading in the pools, surrounded by beautiful scenery and shaded by magnificent foliage; and the water is never too cold. Calipever, hog-nosed mullet, drummers, and snook, are to be found in these rivers, and mountain-mullet in the smaller streams, also eels, shrimps, and cray-fish. I believe that trout would live in some of the cold clear mountain-streams with gravelly bottoms, unless the cray-fish and shrimps destroyed the spawn; at all events, it would be worth the experiment. Black crabs are numerous over the island, and are justly esteemed a great delicacy. They are altogether a different species from the loathsome brute infesting the palisades. The black crab is a vegetable-eating and very cleanly creature, living in the mountains, and only coming down to the sea to spawn. At such times they travel in immense bands, in a direct line, turning aside for no obstacle—not even, it is maintained, for a house! It is contended by epicures that there are four delicacies in Jamaica — viz., the black crab, mountain-mullet, ring-tailed pigeon, and—— I forget the other, but I can answer for the three above mentioned.

The great amusement in Jamaica, and especially for sailors, is riding. At all the northern ports, such as Port Antonio, Ocho Rios, Lucca, or Montego Bay, riding-parties were organised; and oftentimes the skipper, followed by a troop of midshipmen, might be seen galloping through the streets in a cloud of dust, their headlong flight being marked by the cheers of the blue-jackets, barking of dogs, shrieks of women and children, and the squealing of pigs. The horses are small but wiry; and a good gallop into the country, followed by a bathe in the river, a plentiful supply of fresh cocoa-nuts, cigars, and possibly some stronger refreshment, is not to be despised in that country. Our blue-jackets were also very partial to "horse-riding," and some amusing scenes occasionally occurred. On one occasion at Port Antonio, the first lieutenant and I heard a blue-jacket order a horse, and said he to the dusky owner, "I want a very *long* horse." So being requested to select his own steed, he forthwith chose one that seemed longer in the back than the others, and led him away. No sooner was he round the corner than two of his mates, as well as himself, jumped on the unlucky steed, and rode off with much satisfaction.

I had to adjudicate at this place in the case of a collision. A black horse-dealer called to see me, and said his horse had been killed by one of my blue-jackets, and presented his bill for £14. I brought a counter-claim for like amount for damage to the blue-jacket, personal anxiety, &c., &c., and dismissed the man, much to his amazement and disgust; but, having turned the tables upon him, I again investigated the matter on the quarter-deck, when the following evidence was forthcoming :—

The negro said that his horse had been hired by the blue-jacket, and that he had collided with a cart driven by a native. The shaft of the cart had pierced the horse's chest, killing it on the spot.

The facts were not disputed, so it became a question as to who was on the right side of the road. The negro driver swore he was, and the sailor swore he was. The principal witness was a boatswain's mate, who gave his evidence with great clearness as follows :—

"Well, sir, all I knows is that 'Umphreys" (the man's name was Humphreys) "was close hauled on the starboard tack, when this 'ere nigger came a-bearing down on him dead afore the wind. 'Umphreys seeing him a-coming, puts his 'elm down to clear him, but the nigger came right athwart his bows and sunk him. By the rule of the road at sea, sir, 'Umphreys was in the right, and the nigger wrong."

There was a good deal of hard swearing on both sides, and as it was difficult to apply the rule of the road at sea to a landsman, and there was no doubt the man had lost his horse, we gave him £5, and he went away perfectly happy, the value of the animal probably being about £1.

Some very valuable thoroughbred race-horses are bred in the island, a gentleman living near Ocho Rios having a breeding establishment, and importing first-class sires from England to cross with native horses. The Kingston races are well attended, and some very good racing goes on; but the negro jockeys, with a fork tied on to their naked heel, look more like monkeys than human beings.

Towards the end of January 1880 we were ordered away from Port Royal on a round of visits, including Belize, in British Honduras, and Cuba. On this occasion we embarked General Gamble, the Commander-in-Chief of the military stations in the West Indies, Mrs Gamble, and the General's staff.

In addition to this large party, Bishop Tozer, the Bishop of Jamaica, and his chaplain, also took a passage. The Bishop was an old friend and shipmate of mine in years gone by, so I was delighted to welcome him on board. Amongst his personal effects I noticed a long box, apparently containing a salmon-rod, which I was very glad to see, as I was not aware till then that his lordship was a sportsman in addition to his other accomplishments. When we had shaken down in the cabin, I said to the Bishop, "I am so glad you have brought your rod, because I expect we shall get some sport in the Belize river."

"That's not my salmon-rod, my dear Captain," said he; "that's my pastoral staff!"

However, having stowed away the General and the Bishop, with their respective staffs, we made sail to a fine breeze, and reached Belize in four days. The approach to the town is very intricate, and a pilot is necessary, the shoals extending for many miles from the mainland, and a whole day's steaming is occupied before reaching the anchorage. Even then, so shallow is the harbour that a ship drawing fifteen feet water has to anchor some two or three miles from the town.

The town of Belize is built upon a narrow strip of land facing the sea, and occupies both sides of the river of the same name. Immediately at the back of the town is a vast dismal swamp, the home of alligators, snakes, mosquitoes, and sand-flies.

At the time this site for the town was chosen, it was doubtless the best that could be got, for the craft of those days could go into the river to load and discharge their cargoes; but at the present day, ships have to lie a long way outside, owing to the shoalness of the water.

Notwithstanding these disadvantages, Belize is a very important and thriving place. A line of steamers places it in direct communication with New Orleans, from whence it is but four days' steaming.

The fruit trade has made rapid strides of late years, under the able administration of the popular Governor, Mr Barlee (now, alas! no more). The timber trade is also looking up well: in fact, the supply of mahogany and logwood would seem to be inexhaustible. But most of the timber in the immediate neighbourhood having been cut down, the mahogany-cutters have to go a long distance into the forest in search of more. The difficulty of transporting these heavy logs to the water-portage is very great, and the expense increased in proportion; still, as long as the price of mahogany keeps up, it must always be a profitable business.

The Governor's house is a most comfortable one. It used to be surrounded by a swampy jungle; but Mr Barlee had this drained and planted, and transformed it into a beautiful garden, rich in tropical fruits and flowers, with an avenue of cocoa-nut trees facing the sea. Many rare kinds of orchids were to be seen in this garden, some of the old trees being loaded with them.

Talking of orchids, his Excellency the Governor kindly gave me permission to select any for transmission to friends at home. So with the assistance of the gardener I filled several boxes, containing twenty-five specimens in each, and sent them to England, where they duly arrived, and were much appreciated.

Personally, I know nothing of orchids—regarding them merely as parasitical plants of more or less beauty and value; but knowing how much they are valued in England, I sent these on the chance. But my experience goes to show that it is not always wise to send these sort of things without knowing anything about them.

Many years ago I sent a box of Dutch bulbs from the Cape to a friend who owned a fine place in the Midlands. Long afterwards I happened to be in that locality, so I strolled over to my friend's house. He was not at home. The gardener was in the conservatory, and this reminded me of the bulbs. After a short conversation, I inquired if he had ever received any bulbs. "Yes," said the monster; "and d—— the fellow that sent 'em! they was full of redspiders and all sorts of——" I waited to hear no more; but merely remarking, "Ah yes; some idiot, I suppose," &c., cleared out, with a mental reservation not to send any more Dutch bulbs to England.

During our stay the Governor gave a garden-party in honour of our distinguished guests. My old Irish setter Paddy was, of course, of the party escorting his master. Now poor Paddy, who was a setter in Newfoundland, came out as a pointer in the West Indies—his coat being taken off to save him from the heat. He consequently presented a rather ridiculous appearance. One of the Governor's guests, who had been dining rather too freely, was pleased to take notice of Paddy.

"Handsome dog!" said he to me; "but he's not thoroughbred."

"How do you know that?" said I.

"He hasn't enough hair on his hind-legs or belly!" said the critic.

"Well, sir, I expect if my coxwain had been clipping you all the morning, as he has that dog, you wouldn't look very thoroughbred either!" The gentleman retired.

Hearing there was a snipe-marsh at a place called the "Boom," some sixteen miles up the river, I made an expedition there, accompanied by some of the officers. We had a pleasant trip in the steam-cutter, seeing a few alligators and water-tortoises on the way, and reached the Boom about mid-day, only to find the swamp perfectly dry. However, as we had come so far, we determined to stay the night, and try some marshes in the neighbourhood. We were directed to a house where we could get accommodation, and where we passed the night; but the old woman who was to have been our hostess had died the day before, and her corpse was only just removed when we arrived. There were not enough beds for all the party; so Cochrane gallantly volunteered to sleep in the old woman's bed, and a lively time he had of it between fleas and mosquitoes. We none of us had any peace that night, and were glad when morning broke. A bathe in the river much refreshed us, and we started to explore the marshes; but without much success, as the ducks were very wild. Whilst bathing in the river in the evening, the General and party passed down the river on their way back to Belize; so taking a header off the bank, I dived across the river and came up alongside their canoe, to wish them adieu, and that was the last I saw of them.

The water-tortoise, called by the natives

hecatée, is a most curious beast. Our guide brought one for our dinner, and most excellent it was; but before killing it, he showed us the wonderful instinct of the creature, which turned towards the water wherever it was put down, although the water was not in sight, and was a long distance away.

There are a few caymans in the river, but I never heard of their molesting any one; in the harbour sharks are swarming. It would be dangerous even to put one's hand over the side of a boat; and as for bathing, it would be madness. Whilst we were at anchor, an English steamer anchored close by us, and one of the firemen plunged overboard for a bath. It was the last the poor fellow ever had. He never came up again, but the crimson-coloured water told the story of his sad fate.

These sharks afforded us much amusement. We enclosed a 1-lb. tin of compressed gun-cotton in a piece of pork, and lowered it over the side. The torpedo was connected to a battery on the poop, and when the shark turned over to grasp the tempting morsel, the circuit was completed, and off went his head. Notwithstanding what may be said to the contrary, Belize is a healthy place; and although undoubtedly hot, the heat is tempered by the strong sea-breeze during the day.

The presence of a man-of-war is always a welcome sight to the hospitable residents. Unfortunately it is a rare one.

We spent a very pleasant fortnight there, making many friends, and enjoying the kind hospitality of the Governor and Mrs Barlee, and the mercantile community. We visited Belize again in 1882; but I shall reserve any further remarks, and bidding adieu to British Honduras, shape a course for Cuba.

During three successive seasons in the West Indies it was our good fortune to be sent to visit Cuban ports regularly every year. We were therefore able to pick up a little information regarding this fine island. A condensed account I herewith append.

At the time of our first visit, in 1880, the insurrection, which had already devastated the island for eleven years, was almost stamped out, and was confined to the eastern portion. It had not the sympathy of the better class of

Cubans, but was supported principally by discontented blacks, and also by the numerous adventurers bred by the war, who regarded it as a means of enriching themselves by plunder, only surrendering themselves to the authorities on being offered a sufficient bribe.

It was none the less disastrous to the island. Bands of robbers infested the interior, burning sugar estates, mutilating cattle, and levying black-mail on whomsoever they came across. The slaves, of whom there are some 200,000 in the island, as a rule behaved well, merely in some cases offering a passive resistance to work.

From what I could gather, I believe these slaves to be very badly treated. An eyewitness assured me he had seen the negroes working in the fields with bleeding backs, with men standing over them whip in hand, and the overseer riding round armed with revolver and sword. As flogging is not supposed to be practised, the usual manner of punishment is the bastinado, which is applied to the victim in the stocks. He is then kept there till his feet are well, so that there are no marks to show. The law abolishing slavery was promulgated in Madrid on the 16th February 1880; but it is not likely that anything will be done in the matter, beyond the fact that the children born of slaves subsequent to that date will be free. The slave-owners complain that the law, if carried into effect, will ruin them; and the slaves believe that it is only a pretext, and that the institution will be continued under another name.

The financial condition of the island is desperate. The Custom-houses are, and have been for some time, mortgaged to a very large amount. The estimated deficit for the financial year ending 30th June 1880, was calculated at 20,000,000 dollars—probably much below the mark. No taxes are collected, although the treasury is empty, as the people cannot or will not pay, and the authorities dare not make them.

The island is already drained to the utmost by wholesale corruption or gross mismanagement, and will probably gradually drift into bankruptcy. There are about 40,000 troops kept in the country, who are supposed to be paid out of the revenues of the island, and the naval force is supported in like manner; but when it is no longer possible to pay them, they will have to be withdrawn, and the country left to take care of itself.

The city of Havana is a reflex of the condition of the country—an empty treasury, mortgaged Custom-house, officials in arrears, and troops unpaid. The town is infested with adventurers of every nationality. The city, although presenting an imposing appearance from the sea, containing some fine palaces and an opera-house, is badly drained and dirty. The revenues of the country are largely supported by numerous gambling-houses, &c., &c., which institutions are consequently encouraged by the authorities. Of specie there is none,—a dirty paper currency, half the value of gold, being substituted. Murders and robberies are of frequent occurrence; and no redress can be obtained, as the police are generally implicated. The convicts are allowed out of jail to pursue their calling during the night, with the understanding that they return before daylight to share their ill-gotten gains with their jailers.[1]

[1] Shortly before one of our visits to Havana, our Consul-General had been brutally assaulted and very nearly murdered

The harbour of Havana is a very fine one, but owing to the absence of tide, the water is foul and evil-smelling. Thanks to a magnificent climate, the place is not unhealthy in the winter time; but in May, when the rains set in, yellow fever makes its appearance with great regularity.

The tobacco crop was a failure for two years previous to 1880. This was caused by the inordinate use of Peruvian guano, which has been found to be destructive to the plant.

Notwithstanding certain objections which I have touched upon, Havana is a delightful place for a short visit. The opera-house is one of the finest in the world; a military band plays almost every evening in the Plaza. The climate in winter is perfect, and the Spanish officials are most courteous and obliging. A visit to the

by some ruffians. Our visit was opportune, the Spanish authorities believing it to be in consequence of this outrage.

On this occasion the Government officials behaved with great promptitude; several notorious vagabonds had been arrested, and although the real culprits were not forthcoming, the Captain-General offered to hang the lot, *pour encourager les autres*, if the Consul-General would only say the word. The Consul recovered in a marvellous manner, and when I last saw him, was in his usual health.

different tobacco-factories is interesting to those who have never seen the process before (they will probably not care to go a second time). The harbour always presents a gay and busy scene, several steamers arriving and leaving every day, besides sailing-ships from all parts of the globe. A fresh sea-breeze blows all through the day, and the land-breeze at night; but the latter wafts off a most odoriferous bouquet, which one would gladly dispense with.

About forty miles eastward of Havana is the fine city of Matanzas, the third in importance in the island. This place is the cleanest, neatest town in Cuba, as far as my experience goes. None of the objectionable sights which disgrace Havana are to be seen. There are two magnificent clubs and many fine buildings in the town; and at the time of our visit, an exhibition was about to be opened.

A few miles from the city are some wonderful caves, which are well worth seeing. They were only discovered quite accidentally some twenty-five years ago, by a negro who was working on the estate: his crowbar suddenly slipped from his grasp, and disappeared into the earth. The poor fellow, hearing mysterious sounds as the bar descended into the bowels of the earth, ran home, thinking the devil was after him, and told his master. But the fortunate proprietor on whose land they were discovered, has already made a small fortune by exhibiting these caves, which extend for some miles underground. The stalactites are very beautiful; some of them being of a lovely pink colour, and quite transparent—others blue. At one place one comes to a natural grotto, surrounded on all sides with fantastically shaped arches and pillars, and, apparently, a magnificent organ in the corner, all composed of most delicately tinted crystal. About three miles have been opened to the public, and it is probable that much more remains to be discovered.

There is some capital guinea-fowl shooting in the neighbourhood of Matanzas. We made up a party for the purpose, and ascended one of the fine rivers flowing into the bay. Having killed some guinea-fowl and had some refreshment, we wanted to resume the *chasse;* but our guide wouldn't have it. His remarks in

Spanish to a friend, which we happened to overhear, were most amusing. "These English," he said, "are perfect fanatics. They shoot all day in the heat of the sun. I tell them they will have sunstroke. They say, 'We don't care for sunstroke.' They bathe in the river. I tell them they will get the *vomito* [yellow fever]. They say they don't care for the *vomito!* I tell them there are caymans [alligators] in the river. They say they don't care a —— for the caymans or for me either! *Caramba!'* they are mad."

NUEVITAS DEL PRINCIPE

is the seaport of the town of Principe, from which it is distant eighteen leagues. This place was destroyed by the insurgents some years ago, and, like Principe, has suffered much from the war, which has entailed much misery upon the inhabitants. The commercial prospects of Nuevitas are improving, and now that the country is quiet, a considerable revival of trade has taken place.

The principal exports are woods of various

kinds, sugar, honey, bees'-wax, and tortoise-shell. The town is situated at the head of a large salt-water lagoon; this again is connected with the sea by a long winding channel. A pilot is necessary for this channel, on account of the sandbanks on both sides. There is a deep-water passage between. A good anchorage will be found off the town in 15 feet. In taking a pilot at this or any other Cuban port, one must be particular to give the tonnage of the ship according to the *stowage* capacity and not burden, otherwise much confusion will arise, owing to the pilots being paid by tonnage and not draught of water, as they usually are.

There is a curious animal found in this neighbourhood, called the manatee or sea-cow, a kind of herbivorous cetacea. This creature lives in the shallow creeks to be found on the north coast of Cuba, and attains a large size, weighing as much as three or four tons. It is said to be gentle and inoffensive, and the flesh is pronounced to be very similar to pork. It is killed for the sake of its tusks and meat.

NIPÉ (NORTH-EAST COAST).

This is by far the finest harbour in Cuba, easy of access, no dangers, and spacious within. There is no town, or even village, and the place is only inhabited by a few scattered fishermen, who seem very poor, but are doubtless happy and contented in that fine climate. The river Majaré discharges itself into the bay, and is navigable for boats for fifteen miles from its mouth, at which place the town of Majaré is situated. Good shooting is to be had up the river, and in the neighbouring lagoons; and we returned from a very pleasant expedition to the town, with a varied bag of guinea-fowl, flamingoes, ibis, and herons. Our guide or pilot was greatly edified by our shooting birds on the wing, exclaiming, as we knocked over herons, cranes, and other loosely feathered birds, "Pluma no mas!"—Feathers no more! The town of Majaré contains about 2000 inhabitants: the country is well cultivated, some excellent tobacco being grown in the district.

A French company have purchased land in

the neighbourhood of Nipé, with the intention of clearing away the timber and planting sugar and tobacco on an extensive scale.

Deer are very plentiful on the western side of the bay.

The distance from Majaré to Santiago-de-Cuba, the principal city on the south coast of Cuba, is about ninety miles over the mountains, which rise to a height of 7000 feet. A Spanish gentleman told me he often rode this distance in one day on the same horse, a pacer. By starting early and resting during the heat of the day, he and his horse managed the journey without fatigue.

The Spanish pacer moves his two legs on the same side simultaneously: the pace is easy both to man and beast, and the average rate about six miles an hour.

Guantanemo, on the south coast, is also a spacious anchorage, and a fine sporting locality. The town is far removed from the anchorage, and only small ships can anchor off it. The country is regularly hunted by a club, under the management of Mr Mason, our Vice-Consul, who most kindly got up a *chasse* for us, resulting in several small deer, about the size of Scotch roe-deer, being killed; and winding up with a most sumptuous breakfast. Our hurried visit prevented us from enjoying more than one day's sport, but we were promised plenty had we remained.

The climate of Cuba is delightful during the winter months, the heat of the day being always tempered by the fresh sea-breeze. The coast is well lighted, and so well surveyed, that navigating these waters is a perfect yachting trip. The south coast is, like all the islands of the Greater Antilles, much hotter than the north, the trade-wind being cut off by the lofty mountains of the interior, some of them being over 8000 feet high.

INAGUA—BAHAMAS.

This island, although not belonging to the Antilles, being in fact a dependency of Jamaica, may be mentioned here, as it is in close proximity to the north-east point of Cuba. Inagua is a low, flat, sandy island about thirty miles long, covered with low bush; population about 2000, most of whom live at the settlement called "Matthew Town," on the south-west side. A large lagoon called the Salina lies directly at the back of the town, and from this many hundreds of tons of salt have been annually exported. In this Salina were some windmill pumps of American manufacture, of a very clever design. They were so arranged that not only did they face the wind, but also accommodated themselves to its force. By an ingenious contrivance of weights and pulleys acting at the back of the windmill, the apparatus gradually closed itself like an umbrella as the wind increased; and not only that, but each arm or spoke, and there were a great many, also slanted itself sidewise to the prevailing wind. In this way the windmill acted automatically. In a gale of wind it would almost be closed, but would still revolve. As the wind slacked off and the pressure was relieved, the wings would gradually unfold themselves by the weights at the back descending; as the wind again increased, it would lift the weights,—and so on. I daresay these automatic pumps may be seen in many places, but I never saw them before. They seem to do their work well. The salt trade having declined of late years, the works have been to a great extent abandoned, and attention is now being devoted to the planting of cocoa-nuts, which promises to be a very lucrative industry. Land suitable for the purpose can be procured at five shillings an acre. The soil seems to be well adapted for the growth of cocoa-nuts, and a ready market is found in the United States, from which Inagua is only four or five days' steaming. The Atlas Company's vessels touch, to and from New York, once a-fortnight. It must be borne in mind that in cocoa-nut planting no return can be expected for at least six years, after which, with proper care, the trees ought to bear, and average 100 nuts per tree. Allowing 50 trees to the acre, or 5000 to 100 acres, it will readily be perceived that, considering all expenses for purchasing land, plants, labour of planting, fencing, clearing land, and shipping, and reckoning the nuts to be worth £3 per 1000 (the market value in the States), a good margin is allowed for profit. Against this must be considered the risk of hurricanes, disease amongst the trees, the objection to residing in a place like Inagua, the difficulty of finding a responsible agent who understands the business, and the possibility of the demand for cocoa-nuts failing. For these reasons I would scarcely advise any one desirous of emigrating to select Inagua. In the interior of the island is an extensive savannah, where herds of wild cattle, wild horses, pigs, and donkeys roam unmolested. The price of a horse is four dollars, but you must first catch him; of cattle, the same; donkeys, four shillings; pigs, *nil*.

In the winter thousands of ducks and waterfowl of every description congregate in the lagoons and marshes, and afford excellent sport; and in one large lagoon the flamingoes are so numerous that they extend for miles, lining the banks on either side with a roseate fringe. These beautiful birds breed on the island, building their nests on tussocks of grass about two feet from the ground, across which they stride, with their long legs hanging down on each side. Their eggs are collected by hundreds, and are excellent to eat; and their wings are also taken for ornament. The bird itself is rather strong and oily, the young ones only being fit for food.

CARTHAGENA—THE SPANISH MAIN.

After a short spell at Port Royal, we were ordered off on a cruise to Carthagena, under sail; and after a rattling passage, arrived there in three days from Jamaica. This place is the capital of the province of that name, and belongs to New Granada. It possesses the finest harbour on the coast. The town bears traces of ancient grandeur, but is now almost in ruins. The fortifications are of immense thickness and strength, but would be useless against ordnance of the present day. Admiral Vernon, however, found them too much for him, although he made so sure of taking the place that he had a medal struck to commemorate the victory which he never gained. A good deal of the fine harbour is blocked with shoals, so that it is not really so large as it appears. These shoals are supposed to be buoyed; but the buoys are not to be depended on, as the rascally pilots purposely shift them, or remove them altogether, so as to oblige ships to engage their services. We did not do so, but preferred to trust to our own judgment and eyesight; but it is rather risky work, and one might come to grief in this way.

On going ashore to return the Consul's visit, I was astonished by a deafening uproar in the street, apparently two black women fighting and abusing each other, the language being richly interlarded with Spanish oaths. Amongst these cries could be plainly distinguished the screaming of a babe and the soothing tones of a nurse; then again would burst out volleys of abuse, pitched in the highest key. The whole of the above was caused by two green parrots. I bought the pair, and they afforded us much amusement on board for many a day afterwards,—climbing up the rigging, screaming, crying, laughing, and abusing each other, from daylight till dark. I took them to Newfoundland, when we went north; but the cold was too much for them, and one died the first winter, the other some time afterwards. I subsequently bought two others, who are alive and well at this moment; but they have forgotten a good deal of Spanish, and bad language.

Carthagena is a fine bay for boat-sailing, and also for seining. We sent a seining-party away every night; and great fun it was carousing amongst the cocoa-nut plantations that fringed the sandy beaches, or smoking and singing beside enormous bonfires. Every haul of the net brought quantities of fish, from sharks to sardines. There is some shooting in the neighbouring marshes; but the heat is terrific, and I should fancy it would not be altogether healthy work. Every species of insect is represented, and I killed a centipede exactly one foot long, and an inch broad. The temperature was between 80° and 90° all through the day, and this in the winter time. In the summer I should imagine that Carthagena would not be a desirable residence. Its chief merit, in my opinion, is its proximity to the Panama Canal, of which Carthagena may be said to be the key.

I regret that my orders prevented me from again visiting the Isthmus of Panama to see how the canal progressed. The only information I could gather on the subject was from one of the employees, who got occasionally mixed in his remarks. This official had been in the English army, according to his own account, and was one of the survivors of the six hundred! On the occasion of a banquet at Jamaica, he is reported to have thus delivered himself, in concluding a brilliant account of the celebrated charge :—

"And, gentlemen, never shall I forget the enthusiasm which prevailed when the order was given : England expects every man will do his duty"!!!

It is said that so overcome was he with the remembrance of the glorious event, that he then and there sank under the table and remained there till morning.

After ten days pleasantly spent at Carthagena, we prepared for our departure; and having blown up the wreck of a schooner which obstructed the navigation at the entrance to the inner harbour, we sailed on our return to Jamaica.

Head-winds, calms, and contrary currents detained us somewhat on the return trip—the general tendency of the winds, currents, and surface-drift of the Caribbean Sea being towards the land, more especially in the direction of Colon, in the Isthmus of Panama; so that it took us fourteen days under sail to do what we had previously done in three. This opens the question as to what effect the Panama Canal will have upon the tides and currents in the Caribbean Sea. One would naturally suppose that the water in the canal would flow continuously from east to west, or from the Atlantic to the Pacific Ocean, on account of the constant set of the current and the prevailing winds being from that direction. The difference in the height of the tide at Colon and Panama is very remarkable. At the former place the rise and fall of tide is only two or three feet; whereas at Panama the difference between high and low water mark is, as far as I can remember, nearer twenty. The tide is nine hours later at Colon than it is at Panama, so that when it is high or low water at Panama, it is half-tide at Colon.

As a matter of fact, I am inclined to think that in the event of what is called a tide-level canal being cut through the isthmus—that is, a canal without locks, open to the ocean at either end — there would be no continuous stream of water flowing through the canal in any one direction, but the result would probably be that the tides would flow in from either end, meet in the middle, and flow back again, as may be seen in the Straits of Magellan, which, after all, is but a huge canal of Nature's own construction.

It is quite possible that the rush of water may be so great as to seriously interfere with the passage of ships entering the canal, in which case it will be necessary to form a lock at the Panama end; and it may even be necessary, in view of the difference in the depth of the harbours at either end, to slope the bottom of the canal from Colon downwards to Panama. This, according to Max Adler's laughable story,[1] would have the effect of causing the water to flow downhill, thereby draining the Atlantic Ocean into the Pacific!

But, joking apart, the tendency of the water must be to find its own level, and if it can be shown that the mean level of the two oceans is

---

[1] Elbow-Room. By Max Adler.

not identical, there must be a constant flow in the direction of the lowest level.

Now it is not at all certain that the mean level of the Pacific and Atlantic Oceans *is* the same; and it is quite possible that, owing to the rotation of the earth on its axis, and the formation of the land in the neighbourhood of the isthmus, the water may be piled up on the Atlantic side and drawn away on the Pacific side. A glance at the map will show what I mean. And we all know how a strong breeze will keep a river back, or, if in the same direction as the flow of the river, will drive it out of a loch and thus rise the river: so this theory may not be so very absurd after all. I leave it to those learned in such matters.

There is another view of this case which never struck me till now. Geologists are of opinion that at one time the Isthmus of Panama was submerged, and South America an island. They are led to this conclusion by the totally different class of animals to be found on South and North America. At that time the Gulf-Stream, which now warms our shores, must have flowed westward through this channel, and the British Isles were a frozen zone unsuited for human habitation. Cut through the isthmus, and the warm waters of the Gulf-Stream may to a very limited extent be deflected in the direction of their former course. The effect would be probably no more than drawing off a kettle of water from the river Tweed, and the immediate effect upon our climate be imperceptible; but it might to a very trifling extent have some influence—about as much, perhaps, as the endeavour to shampoo an elephant with a single egg! But if I attempt to follow up this subject, I shall get as much mixed as the gentleman before mentioned who led the charge of the gallant six hundred, so I shall not pursue it further. I was led to this diversion from my recollection of the canal scheme twelve years ago, when I was ordered to report upon its feasibility. At that time there were no fewer than five schemes for connecting the Pacific with the Atlantic Ocean. I sorted these schemes, and came to the conclusion that the only one likely to be attended with any success was a direct tide-level canal across the Isthmus of

Panama. I shall be disappointed if this opinion be found not to be correct.

Talking of those days reminds me of a story. At that time the Reindeer, which I commanded, was stationed in the Pacific. We had no parson on board, so a clerical friend of mine volunteered to conduct the service on board one Sunday. Having a purely nautical congregation, the reverend gentleman thought it a fine opportunity to give us a nautical discourse, and he brought his sermon to a conclusion with the following eloquent advice :—

"Now, my men, be guided by me: let not your anchor go on the soft, slippery, and treacherous *mud*, but on the firm and solid *rock*, with the land close aboard under your lee."

Needless to say, this advice was gratefully appreciated by an attentive audience—the poor fellows being always taught to believe that exactly the reverse of this maxim was the object to be desired.

During the passage from Carthagena to Jamaica the following incident occurred :—
" April —, 1880. Lat. —, long. —. Ship under

sail, weather fine and warm. Captain fell overboard. Hove to—lowered a boat—picked captain up—filled and proceeded."

It was currently reported that the skipper had jumped overboard to exercise the crew and to test the merits of a patent lowering apparatus, which, by the by, answered admirably; and there seems to have been some colour for this supposition, seeing that the weather was fine and the water warm. Moreover, no sooner was it known that the captain was overboard than the second lieutenant, followed by two dogs, were also discovered in the water, having gallantly, it is supposed, come to his assistance. Be that as it may, a big shark was observed swimming about, and was speedily caught and hauled on board. This shark belonged to a species known as the ovoviviparous; and being cut open, as sharks always are, to see what they have had for dinner, ten little sharks, about the size of an ordinary cod-fish, were discovered all alive and kicking. The youngsters were thrown overboard, when, sad to relate, another big shark, doubtless the anxious papa, speedily made a meal of them! The poor orphans were thus transferred from the inside of one parent to another. I fear they hardly appreciated the change.

Soon after our return to Jamaica the time came for us to wend our way northwards, and it was not till the following December that we again found ourselves in West Indian waters.

In the early part of January 1881 we were ordered to Haïti to make the round of the island, interview the consuls, and show the British flag.

I took this opportunity of writing a report upon the general features of this most interesting island, embracing the agricultural, financial, political, and social conditions of the country and its inhabitants, but this shall be reserved for another chapter.

HAÏTI AND SAN DOMINGO.

A couple of days' easy steaming against the prevailing north-east trade brought us in sight of the high mountains of Haïti—a description of which island I shall now attempt. I feel sure that the general reader will candidly admit that he (or she) knows nothing whatever about Haïti. I confess that, until my visit to the island, I knew nothing about it, as to what constituted Haïti and what San Domingo. I had heard vaguely of the Black Republic of Haïti, but that is all.

A glance at the map of the West Indies will show the importance of this island, also the boundary-line separating the two Republics of Haïti and San Domingo from each other. Roughly speaking, the whole island is about the size of Ireland—of which one-third belongs to Haïti, a Black Republic speaking French; the remainder to San Domingo, the natives of which are a mixture of white, brown, and black, speaking Spanish.

GENERAL REMARKS ON HAÏTI.

If the island of Cuba be the "Pearl," to Haïti belongs the proud title of the "Queen of the Antilles." Second only to Cuba in size, this magnificent island is second to none in the beauty of its scenery and the fertility of its soil.

The mountains, rising to the height of nearly 9000 feet, are clothed with dense tropical vegetation to their very summits. The valleys are well watered, and are capable of extensive cultivation, and of supporting a numerous population. The whole island embraces about 30,000 square miles; of this 20,000 belong to San Domingo, and 10,000 to Haïti proper.

The total population is roughly estimated at 700,000, of which 200,000 belong to San Domingo and 500,000 to Haïti, which will thus be seen to be by far the more thickly populated of the two countries. Nine-tenths of these 500,000 are pure blacks, the remainder being mostly mulattoes, with a few whites. It is estimated that two-thirds of the whole population are females.

The geographical position of the island is such, that it commands the two most important routes to the West Indies, the Mona and the Windward Passage.

Whoever is in possession of the ports of San Nicholas on the west coast and Samaná on the east, has, in my opinion, the keys to these routes.

The climate of Haïti is much dreaded and abused, probably unjustly so—I believe it to be healthy enough; but the towns, reeking of filth and innocent of drains, are the hotbeds of fever, small-pox, and other noxious diseases. As well might one abuse the climate of Naples because they have the cholera there; forgetting that these scourges are sent to remind us that the ordinary precautions relating to health and cleanliness cannot be neglected with impunity. For this reason Port au Prince, the capital of Haïti, is very unhealthy, especially in the summer months, and ships frequently contract yellow fever by anchoring too close to the shore at this season. In winter time the climate is perfect, and the ports healthy.

The soil, as I shall presently show, is capable of producing every kind of fruit and vegetable, besides the usual tropical productions, such as sugar, tobacco, coffee, chocolate, &c. The forests contain timber of the finest quality; and in the interior, gold, silver, copper, tin, lead, and iron are known to exist; but the mines are unworked, the soil is uncultivated, and the commercial prosperity of the island is paralysed by the jealousy of the Haïtien Government and the fear of foreign intervention. Added to which, the constant revolutions and the gross corruption of the officials have ruined the country financially, and have almost annihilated legitimate trade. I speak more especially of Haïti proper, in contradistinction to that portion of the island styled the Dominican Republic.

I propose to give a short account of each place in the order that we visited them, commencing with the capital, Port au Prince.

Port au Prince, the seat of government, is a considerable town, containing some 20,000 inhabitants, of whom nine-tenths are black, and most of the balance mulattoes. There are very few white British subjects, but several hundred Jamaica negroes, claiming British protection. Most of the mercantile houses are German, or English houses managed by Germans.

Trade is dull, owing to the constant revolutions which disturb the country. There are said to be 8000 troops quartered in the town; but many of these exist only on paper, their

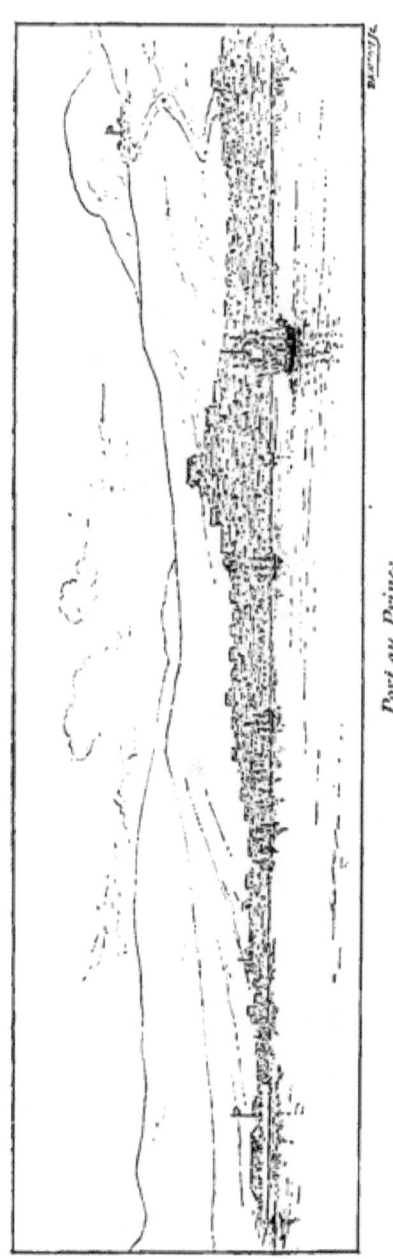

Port au Prince.

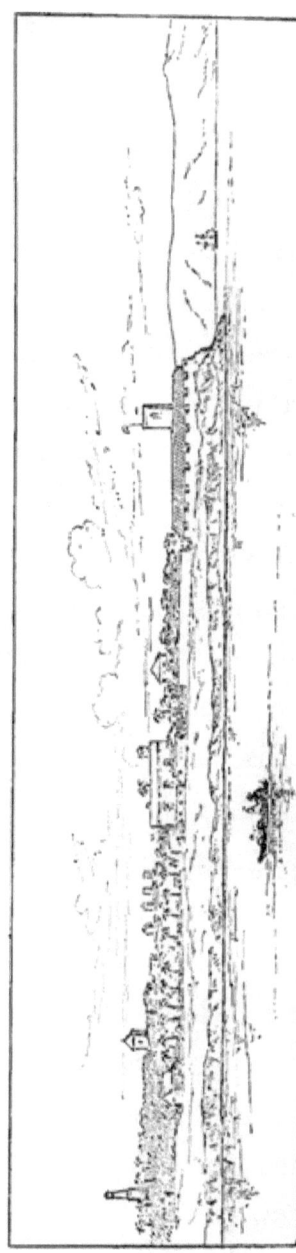

San Domingo.

pay and rations being drawn with great regularity by the numerous generals, of whom there are no less than 2000. Whenever a general dies a salute is fired, consequently minute-guns may be heard almost every day. Many of the titles belonging to Haïtien officials seem to have been borrowed from the confectioners,—thus we have Generals Marmalade and Lemonade, &c.; and the churchyard bears record to the virtues of several noble dukes of the same distinguished character.

The President, General Salamon, is an enlightened and intelligent black man, educated in Paris, with the manners and education of a polished Frenchman. His wife is a French lady of agreeable manners and address.

A grand ball and reception was given in our honour by the President, and all the beauty and fashion of Port au Prince were present. Dancing was kept up with great vigour till an early hour in the morning, notwithstanding that the thermometer stood at 96°. The fun grew fast and furious, and the *bouquet d'Afrique* was decidedly pronounced: naval officers in tail-coats and epaulets swung round with dusky beauties, carrying all before them. Suddenly the trumpets sounded, and the President was announced. The band struck up the national air, and his Excellency was observed approaching, Madame La Presidente leaning on his arm, and a couple of A.D.C.'s on either side—one of them dressed from head to foot in scarlet, with plumes to match, the other in green; so that the gallant old general loomed like a steamer in a Newfoundland fog, with the bow-lights gleaming through the mist. By-and-by supper was commenced; champagne of a very sweet kind flowed like water; speeches followed. The heat and the *bouquet* were awful, but I did not wait to see the last of it, preferring a good cigar in the cool night air outside.

The financial condition of the country may be described as rotten: the Custom-house is mortgaged to a French bank, and all payments are made through the bank. The natives being jealous of foreign interference, no white man is allowed to hold property in Haïti; consequently some of the whites marry Haïtien women and hold property in their name. A considerable trade is carried on from Port au Prince; several lines of steamers regularly call there, and the vessels of the Royal Mail do so once a-month. The town is exceedingly dirty, and during the summer unhealthy, yellow fever and small-pox often raging with terrible malignity. During three months the deaths in Port au Prince alone from the latter disease were *one-fourth of the whole* population.

After a short stay at this place, I took farewell of the worthy old President, who returned the visit, and was received with a royal salute. The sentry at the palace gate asked the first lieutenant, who accompanied me, to give him a copper. The poor wretch was in rags, and probably received no wages.

The President complained much about the disturbed state of the country, but said that his remedies were producing the desired effect. I found out afterwards that he had shot fourteen people at San Marks, and the same number at Cape Haytien. Another fourteen were to have been shot at Gonaives, so that there should be no ill-feeling between the places; but an appeal was made in their favour, and they were brought to Port au Prince and imprisoned instead.

I told his Excellency that we also had our troubles at home, and I wished we had him to deal with the disaffected ones. "Ah," said he, showing his white teeth, "they want a firm grip."

From Port au Prince we proceeded to San Marks, arriving there after dark. The anchorage is deep, close to the shore, so that ships haul their sterns in to anchors on the beach.

San Marks is a thriving little place, with a population of 5000, of whom 30 to 40 are British subjects. About 1500 troops (on paper) are quartered in the town, their pay being drawn by the generals, who receive no pay. A large trade is carried on in logwood, some 12,000 tons of which are shipped annually in French, American, and Norwegian vessels. Eight thousand bags of coffee are also annually exported. A most luxuriant valley extends from the back of the town, estimated to be capable of producing a million pounds of cotton, if it was cultivated. The cotton is of excellent quality, growing almost wild, no plough being used. Pine-apples, strawberries, peaches, melons, oranges, apples, guavas, mangoes, &c., grow wild, without any attempt at cultivation. Tobacco is also grown, but no sugar, the latter being imported.

Our next port of call was Gonaives, a town of some importance, numbering 7000 inhabitants, the only white people being H.B.M. consul and his family.

The town was burnt down in one of the numerous rebellions, and has never recovered. The Bay of Gonaives is spacious, and the scenery in the neighbourhood very fine.

At each of these places it became my duty to pay an official visit to the commandant, who was always a general. Having arranged the time and place, I landed to pay my respects in full uniform, attended by our consul. A ragged guard of honour received me, composed of the most wretched lot of poor half-starved vagabonds. They never had any shoes, and their garments were scanty. A brass band struck up an apology for "God save the Queen," and continued playing it during the interview. After a few preliminary compliments, we adjourned to the *salon*, where a sweet abomination called champagne was served. The general then made a speech overflowing with most fulsome compliments. We then drank her Majesty's health, when it became my turn; and in the best French I was master of, I assured the general of the deep interest her Majesty had always taken in Haïti, and in that place in particular, and trusted that the harmonious relations which had always existed between the two countries would be maintained, &c., &c. After which speech, which required washing down, we again liquored, the Mulligan guards presented arms once more, and we departed.

Rounding the western point of Haïti, the first port of importance is Cape Haytien, commonly called The Cape. This is the second town in Haïti, and may be remembered as the place where H.M.S. Bulldog was abandoned. The city was destroyed by an earthquake in 1843, and subsequently bombarded by H.M. ships Galatea and Lily. At the present time a steam-pinnace with one gun could capture the place. The town is very dirty, being only cleaned by the rains; but the climate is delightful, and the scenery superb. The English consul complained to me that very much of his time, and not a little of his salary, were taken up in burying Jamaica negroes, whose bodies were left lying about the streets. I advised him to send in his bill to the Governor of Jamaica!

Cape Haytien is a port of call for several lines of steamers from Europe and the States. Trade is flourishing, the exports being chiefly coffee and logwood, which are carried in French, German, and Norwegian vessels, but few English. In one year 100,000 bags of coffee, valued at £200,000, and 25,000 tons of logwood, valued at £125,000, were exported. The usual number of paper troops were quartered in the town, commanded by some distinguished general.

We now leave Haïti for a while, but return to it presently. The next port visited by the Druid was Porto Plata, the first place belonging to the Dominican Republic if approaching it from the westward. Hitherto the people have been French-speaking, now they are Spanish— San Domingo having once belonged to Spain, as Haïti did to France. Both are now independent republics.

Porto Plata is a clean, picturesque little town,

superior in every way to the Haïtien ports. The climate is pleasant, and the scenery fine. There are no white inhabitants, beyond the consul and his family. The principal export is tobacco. Sugar is also exported; but the sugar trade is in its infancy, and will probably in time supersede tobacco. Coffee is also a new industry, also cocoa (the chocolate of commerce); honey, bees'-wax, and hides are exported. Very fine mahogany is grown in this district, I saw specimens fully equal, if not superior, to Honduras mahogany. An American company have commenced mining on a large scale, and have started a gold-mine some fifty miles inland. Several shafts have been sunk, and the company expect to net 50,000 dollars per annum. I procured a quantity of earth from the bottom of this mine, containing minute specimens of marine shells,—how they got there I leave to geologists to determine. I have seen marine shells in abundance at the top of a mountain in the Gulf of California, showing that the land must at one time have been covered by the sea; but sea-shells at the bottom of a mine many hundred feet deep is beyond my comprehension. At the city of Santiago de los Caballeros, a day's journey into the interior, a white race of people exist. These people are descended from the old Spaniards, and they do not intermarry or mix in any way with the neighbouring population. Porto Plata possesses a fine iron pier for the convenience of steamers coming alongside, also an iron skeleton lighthouse at the entrance. Our next port of call was Santa Barbara de Samaná, also belonging to San Domingo, one of the most beautiful places in the island, with a snug anchorage; but that is all that can be said for it. The town is a dirty, straggling, picturesque little place, and very unhealthy. During our stay here we exercised at night quarters, but hearing the guns being cast loose, the governor sent off begging us not to create a disturbance, as a revolution would certainly take place. I waited on this functionary in the morning, on behalf of an unfortunate negro, a British subject, whom he had brutally ill-used, and threatened further proceedings if some redress was not given. The poor negroes are very badly treated by these mongrels.

Samaná will one day be a place of importance, as the Americans have an eye on it for a coaling-station, and have been surveying the harbour for some time past. The whole peninsula was at one time ceded to an American company for the purpose of growing fruit, the soil being wonderfully rich and suitable for the purpose; but the contract fell through.

The Custom-house is farmed to a few local merchants, who pay 80 dollars a-day for the proceeds. The money thus gained is supposed to go to pay the troops, who were conspicuous by their absence.

Having now skirted the northern shores of the island, we passed through the Mona Passage, and turned our head westwards, arriving soon afterwards at San Domingo, the capital of the Republic. This city is interesting chiefly to archæologists, the bastions forming a picturesque ruin, and showing traces of former greatness. The city is situated at the mouth of the river Ozama, navigable for craft drawing 11 feet: large vessels have to anchor in the roads, exposed to the wind and sea. It is proposed to dredge the mouth of the river, so as to allow large vessels to anchor off the town. This would increase the commercial prospects of the place to a very great extent. A considerable trade is carried on with European ports. In 1879, 33,400 tons of shipping cleared outwards, carrying cargo of the value of 600,000 dollars. The principal items are sugar, cocoa, gum, hides, honey, bees'-wax, and coffee; also tortoise-shell, mahogany, lignum vitæ, fustic, logwood, and an extract of logwood largely used by wine-merchants for the manufacture of port wine! The imports are about equal in value.

Mahogany is almost exhausted in the neighbourhood, so that it will probably soon cease to be shipped. On the other hand, sugar is being cultivated with success, and is now exported, instead of being imported as heretofore.

Near the borders of a large lake named Enriquillo a mountain of rock-salt has been discovered, and a company has been formed to work the same; but my experience of operations of the kind in countries where revolutions are frequent, would not lead me to be sanguine as to the result of this undertaking. It is said that the lake Enriquillo is connected with the sea, although many miles inland, by a subterraneous passage, and that the water rises and falls with the tide. The Dominican Republic has no standing army; but every man possesses a weapon of some sort, which he freely uses on the slightest provocation. No revolution had taken place for a year previous to our visit, but

Church of San Francisco, San Domingo.

one was confidently expected, and did actually take place very soon afterwards.

The population of the city is about 15,000, two-thirds of whom are of Spanish origin; the remainder are blacks.

The entire navy of San Domingo, a small sailing-schooner, was at anchor off the town.

San Domingo boasts of possessing the oldest church in the New World, built by Columbus. The cathedral, which is unfinished and likely to remain so, contains some fine carvings presented by Ferdinand and Isabella, whose portraits adorn the walls. Columbus's house is also a fine old ruin: the bones of the great

Columbus's House, San Domingo.

navigator have lately been discovered in a box in the church, and are carefully preserved. The discovery was made while excavating near the altar; and from the inscription on the outside of the box, as well as that on a silver plate on the inside, there seems to be strong reason to believe that they are the remains of the great man — at least part of them, for the Spaniards claim to have already got his remains at Havana, having abstracted them from this very church. It is said, however, that they have been imposed on. Meantime each party regards the other as an impostor. From very careful inquiries, I gathered that these parties have got between them three or four tons of bones belonging to Columbus, including at least three of his skulls. One of his skeletons is also preserved at Genoa.

Leaving San Domingo on the 24th January, we once more crossed the boundary and entered Haïtien waters at Jacmel. Interesting as were all these places, I consider Jacmel to bear the palm as the most interesting of them all. It is rather a handsome-looking town from the sea, and boasts some fortifications. Observing these, I sent ashore to ask if a salute would be returned if we fired one. I was told they would certainly do so if we would lend them the powder, as theirs had all been expended in firing minute-guns for departed generals. So we lent them the powder, and at the same time borrowed a Haïtien flag wherewith to salute.

I am not sure who was in the more humiliating position of the two. The officials of the port came off in full dress, to thank me for the honour. There is something touching in these poor fellows endeavouring to keep up appearances for the credit of their country, appearing in gorgeous uniforms, smothered in gold lace, when one knows that they have not received any pay for a twelvemonth, nor had a square meal for as long; that at their own home they live on any garbage, and dress in the seediest of garments, and keep their family in a state of semi-starvation, to pay for their uniform and the trappings of their charger.

I have said that Jacmel is an interesting place, and so it is. The town is the filthiest I ever saw—even in Haïti. Manufactures there are none. Agriculture in the most primitive state—in fact, left much to nature; the coffee-plants grown into trees, and the berries dropping on the ground. The soil is splendid, but the people are too indolent to develop it; provisions are consequently scarce and dear. There are 800 troops (visionary) quartered in the town, and no less than 300 generals, of whom only 10 are paid : the remainder forage about and get their living as they can. There is a hospital, but it is roofless: no charitable institutions of any kind exist—no refuge for the poor, sick, or blind. Lunatics roam at large.

There are no British residents except the consul : it is very much to his credit that he is not a lunatic also. The place is very unhealthy, and steamers generally give it a wide berth.

I shall have more to say of Jacmel presently; but I shall move on for the present to the last port of call in Haïti—Aux Cayes, a very pretty little town, and a good anchorage, although an open roadstead. The population numbers 10,000, none of whom are white, except the consul, his family, and a few merchants. A considerable amount of trade is done here, and several lines of steamers call regularly for cargoes. The principal exports are—coffee, honey, cocoa, and logwood. The Government, with short-sighted policy, lately increased the duty on logwood, thereby putting a prohibitory tax upon it, with the object of preventing foreigners from making a living, and thus driving them out of the country in disgust. The environs of Aux Cayes are beautiful, and there are very pretty rides about; but the hopeless condition of the roads renders any exercise of the kind more a toil than a pleasure.

CHAPTER XV.

REMARKS UPON THE SOCIAL AND RELIGIOUS INSTITUTIONS OF HAÏTI.

It would be impossible to dismiss Haïti without something more than a passing glance at the social and religious condition of this remarkable island—a condition of affairs so peculiar, that I shall neither be surprised nor offended if the reader gives me credit for a lively imagination, or at least a gross exaggeration of facts. All I expect is a careful perusal of the forthcoming chapter, and the reader may believe it or not as he pleases.

On our first arrival at Port au Prince, I was informed by a gentleman in high position and undoubted integrity that I had come amongst a race of people indulging in cannibalism, secret poisoners, sorcerers, ghouls, child-slayers, and serpent-worshippers, This information was imparted to me in a mysterious way—with doors closed and bolted, and a careful look round to see that no cavesdroppers were about. My informant assured me that if it was known that he was telling me of these matters, his life would not be worth an hour's purchase, as he would be undoubtedly poisoned; but that he felt it his duty to apprise me, as a naval officer in command of one of her Majesty's ships, of these proceedings.

Having listened to a mass of disgusting details sufficient to sicken a scavenger, I went on board and pondered over them, aided by a cigar and some mild refreshment. "Either these things are facts or false," I said to myself; "they may be the distorted imagination of an intellect deteriorated by long residence in such a place, or they may be perfectly true; at any rate, as I am going round the island, I will endeavour to find out." Taking counsel of my trusty first lieutenant, we made careful inquiries at every place we visited in Haïti, from those competent to judge of the truth of these matters; and although information was not readily forthcoming—especially from the blacks—still, when we assured people that anything they might say would be considered confidential, and that their names would not be exposed, a good deal of interesting details were divulged, corroborating to a remarkable degree the particulars already detailed to me.

Before going further, it will be necessary to explain how the island came to be peopled by the present inhabitants.

It seems that the ancestors of the present inhabitants of Haïti came originally from the Congo, on the west coast of Africa. They are said to have belonged to a race called the Mondongoes. These people are cannibals and serpent-worshippers; they are also sorcerers, and famed for their skill as secret poisoners. The descendants of this race brought with them to Haïti all the arts and secrets of their religion. During the French occupation they appear to have been debarred from practising their rites; but since the French evacuated the island, some eighty years ago, they have indulged in them, and continue to do so at the present time. The religion of Haïti is ostensibly Roman Catholic: an archbishop, four bishops, and nearly one hundred priests of that order are established in the country; but they are powerless in the face of a secret society called the Voudoux or serpent-worshippers, which pervades all classes of the blacks from the President downwards. The present head of the Republic, General Salamon, a black man, is professedly averse to Voudouxism; but as his position depends upon his influence with the blacks, he is neutral in the matter, and prefers to ignore it.

The immediate effect of Voudouxism has been disastrous to the country. Trade is paralysed, and the natural resources of the island remain undeveloped. Haïti is known to possess valuable mines of gold, silver, and copper, which are not worked. Hundreds of thousands of acres of virgin soil, capable of producing the finest crops of sugar, coffee, tobacco, cocoa, and indigo, are neglected. The population is reported to be decreasing; the mortality amongst children is alarming; and deaths by secret poisoning and assassination are frequent. That this is due to the influence of Voudouxism there can be no doubt.

Priests belonging to the order are to be found in every village, and temples for the practice of their diabolical rites and ceremonies are scattered over the country. At these places, at regular times, corresponding with our Christmas, Easter, and Whitsuntide, the most disgusting orgies and sacrifices take place. No white man has ever been permitted to witness these ceremonies; but from trustworthy evidence I am able to furnish the following details.

The people are called together by beat of drum, usually at midnight. The ceremony begins by administering oaths enjoining secrecy. Dancing then commences, the excitement being supplemented by copious libations of rum, till one or more of the wretches fall down in a fit, when the spirit of Voudoux is supposed to have entered into them. These orgies generally last three days, but often much longer. On the first night a priest sacrifices a cock at the altar, the blood being drunk warm. Dancing then recommences, and the orgies go on till the individuals are incapable of further exertions. On the second night a goat is sacrificed, and the blood drunk as before. On the third night the orgies continue, when a little child is brought in: the child's throat is cut by the priest, the blood handed round and drunk warm; the body is then cut up and eaten raw, that which is not disposed of being salted for further use, special parts being reserved for the priest. The women are said to be the worst on these occasions. Children not over ten years of age are usually selected for sacrifice, those of pure African descent being preferred. It is said that such is the fear of the priest that as many children as are required are invariably forthcoming—either given up, often voluntarily so, by their own mothers, or stolen. A class of professional child-stealers exist, whose business it is to supply the victims. These monsters, generally women, enter a house during the night, their bodies naked and oiled, and steal the child. The unfortunate victim is then rendered insensible by narcotic poison and kept in a secret place till required, when it is restored to consciousness by antidotes, preparatory for the final sacrifice. In this manner it is computed that many hundreds of children are annually butchered. So great is the dread of the Voudoux priests, that no complaint is made by the parents, and it is even stated that mothers have been known to fatten up their own children for the sacrifice! No wonder that the mortality amongst children is great.

But it is not only on these occasions that children are devoured; the negro would appear to have a natural relish for human flesh, and women have been known to eat newly born children. Human flesh has been sold in the markets, and it is said that a lard is prepared from human fat and sold in the same way. Instances have occurred of both men and women being caught in the act of eating children they have killed in cold blood, not because they were starving, but from taste. In these cases the guilty parties have received a mere nominal punishment, to satisfy public opinion. In the days of President Geffrard, Voudouxism was suppressed with a strong hand; and on one occasion, when it was proved that a child had been stolen, murdered, and eaten in the name of Voudoux, the guilty parties, eight in all, among whom were several women, were tried and publicly shot. It is, however, generally admitted that this act of justice was utterly without effect, except that it made the practice more secret; and the condition of the country is acknowledged to be in this respect worse than ever. But these things, horrible though they are, sink into insignificance beside the fact that it is by no means an uncommon occurrence for corpses to be disinterred in order to feast upon the putrid remains. Lest this may not be credited, I may mention here that, at the time of our visit to Jacmel, two negroes were caught eating a corpse they had disinterred and stolen. They were sentenced to a month's imprisonment and thirty dollars' fine!

To show that these statements are not pure inventions but are founded on fact, I will here give a few extracts from notes taken on the spot.

In May 1878 two women were caught at Port au Prince in the act of eating a female child. It was proved that the child had been purposely drugged by these wretches. The poor parents, believing it to be dead, had it buried, when these women disinterred it, restored the poor child to its senses by antidotes, then killed it in a most cruel way and ate it.

A Haïtien and his family were discovered eating a small boy, another boy being tied to a tree ready to be devoured. These people were shot. Human meat has been openly sold in the market-place of Port au Prince and identified by a medical man. At San Marks Voudouxism is in full operation, especially in the mountains. The people assemble at beat of drum, as already described; many children are sacrificed, and human flesh has been sold in the market-place by the barrel under the name of pork. This was told me by an eyewitness who recognised the flesh.

Corpses are disinterred for food and robbery. The Government are aware of these proceedings, but wink at them.

Gonaives.—Voudouxism exists here, but in a modified degree; the feasts and ceremonies take place in the town, but no human sacrifices. In the country the same customs prevail as elsewhere. My informant, having black blood in his veins, was somewhat reticent.

Cape Haytien.—Voudouxism is principally confined to the mountains; the ceremony commencing with the sacrifice of cock, goat, or serpent, and ending with children—a three days' debauch. A clergyman of the Church of England, himself a coloured man, told me that Voudouxism interfered greatly with his work. He substantiated the horrible atrocities perpetrated along the coast and in the country; children stolen, butchered, and their flesh sold in the town. He said that a woman offered human flesh for sale at his own door, and that his wife was nearly buying it, believing it to be pork.

Jacmel.—The hotbed of Voudouxism. The ceremony was described to me by an eyewitness, who saw the human remains eaten, and probably participated in the feast.

Two men in prison for eating a child, caught red-handed and fined. Two others caught eating a corpse. At Christmas time gigantic orgies took place, lasting a fortnight. It was computed that 9000 persons were present, the rendezvous being at the house of a notorious Voudoux priestess named Susanette.

At Aux Cayes Voudouxism is said not to be so bad; but the annual feasts are the same, as certified by reliable eyewitnesses, one of whom was present at the baptism of a woman for the Voudoux faith. Before being permitted to join this sect, it is said to be necessary for the candidate to have murdered some one, either black, brown, or white—children for choice; hence it would appear that nine-tenths of the whole population of Haïti are murderers as well as cannibals, since nearly every man or woman belongs to the sect.

As a matter of fact, it is not too much to say that one portion of the community are engaged in devouring the other. It is hardly surprising that under this process the population should decrease. In the art of secret poisoning the Voudoux priests are said to be unusually expert: the secret was brought over from their native land, and transmitted from father to son. They are said to be familiar with the properties of every tree and shrub, and their effect upon the human system; and they claim that as professional poisoners they have no equal.

In this matter of secret poisoning I confess it was very difficult to obtain any information, so tenacious are they of the secrets of their infamous trade. The Voudoux priests are professional poisoners in addition to their other accomplishments: they exercise their vocation with great secrecy and success, and so craftily that detection is impossible. It is said that these wretches can poison by slow degrees or quickly; that they can deprive a person of reason either temporarily or permanently, with or without pain, as desired; that they can cause the victim to break out with loathsome eruptions, or reduce a person to a state of insensibility resembling death, and restore him at will by the use of antidotes. For every known poison they have the antidote, and in fact there seems to be no limit to their cunning and their skill. In consequence they are often applied to by persons desirous of ridding themselves of an enemy, from motives of envy, hatred, or revenge; especially, also, by women desirous of "removing" an importunate lover, or one who has deserted them for another.

The above, doubtless, accounts for the mysterious disappearance of persons so frequent in Haïti.

Sorcery is also practised all over the country; every black man or woman is a firm believer in it, and there are schools for the study of this art. In this respect the Jamaica blacks are equally ignorant and superstitious. They are all believers in "Obie"-worship, which is identical with Voudoux; and I am of opinion that the same ceremonies and orgies would be practised in Jamaica as in Haïti, were it not for the strong arm of the law.

It may be said, What are the Roman Catholic priests doing to permit such atrocities, seeing that the religion of the country is professedly Roman Catholic? The fact is, they are powerless in the matter: they are perfectly aware of the proceedings, but, being unable to prevent them, they wink at or openly countenance them. As a matter of fact, the Roman Catholic religion is not that of the country, but is assumed to keep up their position in the eyes of civilised nations. Theirs is what it always has been—the religion, if it can be called one, of the West African negro,—an unwholesome mixture of sorcery, murder, cannibalism, secret poisoning, and corpse-eating. Such is the religion of Haïti; and such it is likely to remain, whatever may be said to the contrary, until civilised nations step in and exclaim that the time has arrived when God's beautiful world shall no longer be defiled by such savages as these. The land should be taken from them and given to a people more worthy to hold it, and to utilise the many advantages a bountiful Providence has enriched it with. An example should be first made of the Voudoux priests, who make a living by imposing on the ignorance of the poor black savages.

Better had it been if Columbus had never discovered these islands, or, having done so, had left the simple harmless race who then inhabited them in possession, instead of allowing his people to brutally ill-use and eventually destroy them, only to be replaced by such barbarians as these. Philanthropists may claim that the black man is intellectually equal to the white, and equally capable of self-government. I think that after such revelations as I have attempted to describe, it is an insult to one's intelligence to suppose so.

In answer to this the Haïtiens may point to their institutions, schools, churches, and laws, modelled, as they claim, after those of France (no compliment to the latter country, by the by), and to their diplomatic relations with other civilised countries. They claim also that life and property are safe. As regards the former it is probably so, provided the traveller be old and tough; as regards the latter, no foreigner is allowed to hold land in his own name: but I believe it is admitted that the ordinary traveller may go where he pleases without fear of being molested.

These people (the Haïtiens) have their faults, and their tastes are certainly peculiar; but their faults are due to ignorance, and I believe the poor uneducated inhabitants are naturally peaceable and honest.

It is difficult to conjecture what will be the future of Haïti; possibly in time to come it may be annexed by the United States or other powerful and civilised country. In the meantime it is, I fear, destined to remain a blot on the face of the earth, a disgrace and a parody on the name of civilisation, and a monument of anarchy and misrule.

It was without any regret that we turned our backs upon this beautiful island and its ghastly horrors, and returned to Jamaica, preparatory to further service on the coast of Newfoundland.

In the introduction to Sir Spencer St John's interesting book on Haïti [1] (which I have only seen while my book is going through the press), I notice the following extract :—

"After having written the chapter on Voudoux-worship my attention was called to a communication which appeared in 'Vanity Fair' of Aug. 13, 1881, by a reply published in a Haytien journal. It is evident that the writer in 'Vanity Fair' was a naval officer, or a passing traveller in the West Indies, and he probably carefully noted the information given him. He was, however, too inclined to believe what he heard, as he gravely states that a Haytien told him that the kidneys of a child were first-rate eating, adding that he had tried them himself; and the writer remarks that the Haytien did not seem to think it

---

[1] St John's 'Black Republic.'

strange or out of the way that he had done so. No Haytien would have ever stated seriously that he had eaten human flesh. Probably amused by the eagerness of the inquirer, he told the story to test his powers of belief, and must have been diverted when he found that his statement was credited. Cannibalism is the one thing of which Haytiens are thoroughly ashamed.

"This communication makes mention of the herb-poisonings and their antidotes; of the midwives who render new-born babes insensible, that are buried, dug up, restored to life, and then eaten. In May 1879 a midwife and another were caught near Port au Prince eating a female baby that had been thus treated; he adds that a Haytien of good position was discovered with his family eating a child. In the former case the criminals were condemned to six weeks' imprisonment, in the latter to one month. (I may notice that I never heard of a respectable Haytien being connected with the cannibals.) The light punishments inflicted were due to the fear inspired by the Voudoux priests. In January 1881 eight people were fined for disinterring and eating corpses. An English medical man purchased and identified the neck and shoulders of a human being in the market at Port au Prince. In February 1881, at St Marc, a cask of so-called pork was sold to a foreign ship. In it were discovered fingers and finger-nails, and all the flesh proved to be that of human beings. An English coloured clergyman at Cap Haïtien said that the Voudoux did away with all the effect of his ministry; and that his wife was nearly purchasing in the market human flesh instead of pork. Four people were fined in that town for eating corpses. When the writer arrived at Jacmel he found two men in prison for eating corpses; and on the day of his arrival a man was caught eating a child. Near the same town nine thousand people met at Christmas to celebrate Voudoux rites. At Les Cayes a child of English parents was stolen, and on the thieves being pursued, they threw it into a well and killed it.

"These are the statements made by the writer in 'Vanity Fair,' and *nearly all are probable*. If correct, the open practice of Voudoux-worship and cannibalism must have made great strides since I left Hayti, and shows how little a black Government can do, or will do, to suppress them. The digging up and eating of corpses was not known during my residence there.

"This communication to 'Vanity Fair' provoked a reply in a journal published at Port au Prince, called 'L'Œil,' October 1st, 1881. It denies everything, even to the serious existence and power of the Voudoux priests, and spends all its energies in abuse. The article is quite worthy of the editor, who was one of the most active supporters of President Salnave, whose connection with the Voudoux was notorious. It is in this angry spirit that the Haytiens generally treat any public reference to their peculiar institution."

I read this extract with the greatest possible interest; for in it I traced my own handwriting, word for word, taken from original notes. As a matter of fact, it is doubtful if these notes would ever have been published, even in the modified form they are here presented; but since they have been already published by a friend to whom I lent them, and since Sir Spencer St John not only confirms my account, but, from his long experience of the country, gives fuller details, there can be no possible object in withholding them now. It will be observed that Sir Spencer allows the probability of the statements in 'Vanity Fair,' excepting the fact of any Haïtien admitting that he had eaten human flesh. Now this, as well as every other statement I have mentioned, is perfectly true. On the occasion referred to I was in conversation with a black man, and happened to mention cannibalism in a random kind of way, as though I had not heard anything about it. On my asking him if he ever indulged in anything of the kind, he promptly denied doing so. I turned the conversation, but just before leaving him alluded to it again, in a light and airy way, leading him to suppose I rather hankered after the institution myself.

"Well, captain" (the fellow spoke English perfectly), " all I know is, a child's kidneys is first-class, though some says the knuckles is better!" Possibly he may, as Sir Spencer says, have been joking; but from the way he smacked his lips and showed his teeth, I should say the joke was rather a ghastly one. This reminds me of the story of a missionary, lately returned from the west coast of Africa. Being asked by a lady "How he liked babies?" replied, "Well, mum, on the whole, I prefer them boiled!"

CHAPTER XVI.

A CRUISE AMONGST THE ISLANDS OFF THE MOSQUITO COAST—THE BAY ISLANDS—BELIZE AND GRAND CAYMAN.

ON the 29th April 1882 the Druid left Jamaica on a cruise to break the monotony of swinging round a buoy in Port Royal harbour. Our destination had been left entirely to my option by an indulgent commodore; so the ship's head was pointed for the island of Old Providence, on the Mosquito Coast. To explain the reason of this, I must go back to the year 1878, when I happened to be on the Isthmus of Panama on my way home from the South Pacific. At this time Mr Malet, our consul at Panama, told me a curious story. He said that a native of Nassau had been to him with some old Spanish coins, bearing date 1625, which he said he had discovered in a cave in the island of Santa Catalina—an appendage to Old Providence. The man—Curry by name—also produced some precious stones in the rough and other curious relics, which he declared he had obtained at the same time. His story was, that whilst wooding and watering a small schooner which he commanded, he saw an iguana, or large lizard, and chased it. The creature escaped into a crevice in the rocks: he followed, and found that the place had been bricked up. On removing the bricks he found a cavern, into which he crawled; and after his eyes had become accustomed to the darkness, he found himself in a spacious vault, with jars on either side and packages lying about. On opening these, he discovered them to be filled with doubloons, half and quarter doubloons, golden crucifixes, and precious stones. Curry went on to say that, having filled his pockets with as much as he could carry, he returned on board, intending to make a second expedition; but that, on attempting to land, he was driven off by the natives. He there upon sailed away to Colon to seek further assistance, and reported the matter to the consul. Mr Malet told me that, however improbable the man's statement was, he could not do otherwise than believe it, after the evidence he produced in the shape of plunder. This caused a considerable excitement on the isthmus at the time; but, being homeward bound, I thought no more of the matter. However, on my arrival in the West Indies the following year, I again became interested in the story—especially as Curry was then living in Jamaica.

What lent a colour to the yarn was the well-known fact that Morgan, the celebrated buccaneer, had amassed enormous wealth in those seas—notably at the sacking of Panama, when he and his gang brought over to Chagres no fewer than 175 mule-loads of gold, silver, and jewels. A mutiny taking place, the spoil was divided. Morgan retired to Jamaica with his share — 400,000 "pieces of eight." He then quitted the buccaneering trade, retired into private life, bought a plantation in Jamaica, and lived on it; and so thoroughly did he recommend himself to public favour, that he was knighted, and appointed governor of the island.

What became of the balance of the spoil, history does not record; but it is supposed to have been hidden upon the numerous islands off the Mosquito Coast, of which Catalina is one.

Several of Morgan's followers were subsequently caught and hanged at Port Royal. One of the most notorious, Captain Kidd, is said to have offered his weight in gold on condition that his life would be spared. The offer was not accepted, and his secret died with him.

I interviewed Curry on several occasions. He invariably swore to the same story, producing a plan of the island of Santa Catalina: and he declared that he was ready to go with me at any time and show me the place; adding that I might shoot, hang, or flog him—which I said I would certainly do—if he failed to carry out his part of the agreement.

Curry estimated the treasure at a fabulous amount; and there were not a few—myself amongst the number—who believed that his story must have some foundation; for there was no disputing the fact that he was possessed, either by fair means or foul, of considerable wealth for a man in his position. In consequence of these rumours, several expeditions were made to Catalina by adventurers of every degree — amongst whom were doctors, Jews, parsons, and others—but all to no purpose, as Curry very wisely declined to accompany them, always declaring he would not go except in a man-of-war.

Being anxious to test the truth of the story, I repeatedly urged the commodore to allow me to visit the island in the Druid; but was always flatly refused by two successive commodores, the terms pirate, filibuster, and buccaneer being applied to my name. Notwithstanding these repeated rebuffs, I never lost sight of the matter, regarding it as an interesting problem to solve, and a pleasant trip to make; for I had long since, by means which it is not necessary here to describe, ascertained that the story circulated by Curry was an audacious fabrication, although I could not account for his having the coins in his possession. Up to the last Curry swore he was ready and willing to accompany me; but at the last moment he failed, as I felt certain he would, and so it came about that we sailed without him.

Three days of pleasant sailing brought us in sight of Old Providence, and rounding the southern point of the island, we anchored on the lee side of Santa Catalina, im-

Catalina Island. Morgan's Head.

mediately off a remarkable rock called Morgan's Head, from the resemblance to the head of a man. Catalina is connected with Old Providence by a narrow neck of land, over which the tide flows at high water.

There is no doubt that these islands were the

headquarters of the buccaneers, and from them they made expeditions to cut out the Spanish galleons on their way from Panama and the Spanish Main. The ruins of a fort were plainly visible, and several old guns were lying in the water at the foot of it. Catalina is uninhabited; but is partially cultivated by the people living in Old Providence. The present population of the island is about 500 : they are white or nearly so, and are descended from the old buccaneers, as their names would imply. The principal man's name is Hawkins, that of a well-known freebooter. The people all speak English, and are of English extraction. These islands belong to the United States of Columbia : a prefect and a few soldiers live on the neighbouring island of St Andrews. The inhabitants of Old Providence seemed greatly amused at the interest taken in their island in consequence of Curry's fiction; and they showed us some amusing documents from persons of position in Jamaica, offering to share profits with any one discovering the treasure, and giving bogus bonds for fabulous sums in return. Stirred up by these reports, the natives prosecuted a search, and one of them actually found a jar full of doubloons at the bottom of a well. I saw the man, but of course he would not say where he found it or the amount; but as he was able to build a house and purchase a schooner out of it, it must have been considerable. I have no doubt plenty more is stowed away amongst the ruins of the fort. Needless to say we found none, although a diligent search was made by some of our party.

Both Old Providence and Catalina are mountainous and partially cultivated: the climate is healthy, and the trade-wind blows fresh all the year round. We spent a very pleasant time bathing and hauling the seine on the sandy beaches, or smoking and reposing under the shade of the cocoa-nut plantations.

The principal trade is in cattle, cotton, cocoa-nuts, and tortoise-shell. Many hawksbill turtles, the tortoise of commerce, are caught on the neighbouring *cays*, and a smart trade is carried on with the United States. Altogether these folk manage to make out a tolerably easy existence, with the help of an occasional wreck, which an incompetent or a rascally skipper throws in their way. Catalina is covered with a villanous plant, called the cockspur-tree, on account of the terrible spurs or thorns with which it is armed. Not only is this tree formidable in itself, but it is invariably swarming with a vicious species of ant about three-quarters of an inch long. If you accidentally touch one of these trees, the ants drop on to you: a hasty retreat to the water is then desirable. There are a few pigeons in the islands, and ducks frequent them in the rainy season.

After three or four days pleasantly spent at these islands, we proceeded northwards, and threading our way through many dangerous reefs, shaped a course for Swan Islands, which lie directly in the path of ships going from Jamaica to Belize. They are so insignificant as to be scarcely marked on an ordinary atlas, and are but little known and seldom visited. I was therefore desirous of exploring them. Running along the south side of the islands, we anchored in a sandy bay on the west side, where we observed a small settlement. We found three Americans living here, acting on behalf of the Pacific Guano Company. The islands are entirely composed of phosphate of lime, a valuable guano. It is as hard as rock, and the colour of cocoa, and has to be crushed by machinery. Thousands of tons of phosphates have been taken off the west island in former years, but operations are suspended, and the plant—*i.e.*, the tramway, trucks, &c.—has fallen into decay. The poor fellows thus doomed to solitary exile devote themselves to agriculture on a small scale. Cocoa-nuts thrive luxuriantly, also bananas, melons, pumpkins, and sweet-potatoes. The delight of these poor folks at seeing a man-of-war may be imagined. They could not do too much for us: everything they possessed was at our disposal, and, in return, we supplied them with the latest papers, flour, tea, tobacco, and suchlike luxuries. There are no springs on the island, but rain-water is collected in cisterns; consequently every creature —bird, beast, or reptile—has to come to these tanks to drink. There are thousands of blue bald-pate pigeons, a few semi-wild hogs, and numerous iguanas on the island. We devoted a day to the chase, bagging over 400 pigeons, and some hogs. Logger-head turtle come ashore at night to lay their eggs. We captured some of them, but they are coarse eating: the eggs are excellent.

The east island is as rich in phosphates as the other, and has never been worked; but there is no anchorage off it, and landing is at all times difficult.

Many kinds of wood abound, some of great value, such as ebony, sandal-wood, and plum. A very poisonous tree, called Manchioneal, is common in the woods, and care should be taken to avoid it. The leaves or juice, if rubbed on the skin of man or beast, causes a blister, and is not easily cured. It is said to be dangerous to sleep under the shade of this tree; and if an animal be tied to one of this description, and it should come on to rain, the drippings would probably kill or seriously injure it. I once saw a donkey that had been almost flayed in this way.

Our visit was quite a godsend to the poor islanders; and when we made sail from the anchorage, the "stars and stripes" were hoisted and dipped, and a gun fired, in grateful remembrance of our visit.

From Swan Islands we shaped a course for

Bonacca, one of the Bay Islands in the Gulf of Honduras; and the next morning the high land of that island was in view.

The Bay Islands consist of three—Bonacca, Routan, and Utilla—Bonacca being the most easterly one, the others lying to the westward in the order named. An extensive coral-reef surrounds the group, and caution is necessary in approaching it, as the reefs are not all marked on the chart. Running along the outer edge of the reef surrounding Bonacca, we steered through a gap and dropped our anchor in the clear smooth water inside.

The island of Bonacca is mountainous and heavily timbered, but only the low-lying lands are capable of cultivation. It may be likened to a round-topped hat, only the brim of which is fertile. On this part cocoa-nuts, bananas, mangoes, and pine-apples thrive luxuriantly, and a considerable trade in fruit is carried on with New York and New Orleans, several steamers and clipper schooners being engaged in the trade. The main island is so infested with a venomous fly that it is impossible to live on it. The inhabitants are obliged to live entirely on the outlying *cays*, or small islets, which are free from these pests. The natives have built substantial wooden houses on the *cays*, and planted cocoa-nut trees, so that they present a very pleasing and picturesque appearance. At the time of our visit some 546 souls were living on the *cays*. The barrier-reef unites all these *cays*

Sheen Cay, Bonacca Island.

together, forming a perfect anchorage inside. I had intended remaining only twenty-four hours at Bonacca; but the simple natives begged so hard for us to stay over Sunday, that I decided to remain, and thus give them the rare opportunity of attending divine service on board an English man-of-war. These people are all British subjects, and speak nothing but English. I had no cause to regret acceding to their request, for we enjoyed our stay immensely. The beautiful sandy bays and shady cocoa-nut groves were a source of endless pleasure. We bathed, gathered shells, hauled the seine, and revelled in cocoa-nuts, mangoes, and pine-apples to our hearts' content; and in the quiet evenings the girls sang and played to us with simple taste and pathos—"God save the Queen" and "Home, sweet home" being among the most popular airs. One very pretty brunette, named Evangeline, the daughter of a worthy old Scotchman, was decidedly the belle. I crowned her with a wreath of pretty pink shells, and christened her the Princess of Bonacca.

On Sunday the ship was thronged, and given up entirely to the people. Besides our usual Sunday service, we had seven weddings, and no less than twenty-four christenings, so our chaplain had a busy time. The babies were lively, and the consumption of sweet biscuits and preserved fruits enormous. Every one was anxious to be married under the British flag; and I believe if we had prolonged our stay, there would not have remained a *single* person on the island. With universal lamentations we bade adieu to this lovely island and its simple inhabitants, and bore away for Routan, and after narrowly escaping a reef not marked upon our charts, anchored there the same evening. Before going further, it will be necessary for me to explain the situation of the inhabitants of these islands.

The Bay Islands originally belonged to Great Britain, and were populated by British subjects emigrating from Jamaica and Grand Cayman. In the year 1859 they were ceded to the Republic of Honduras. The immediate cause of this was the proposed railway from Port Cortes on the Atlantic coast, to Fonseca Bay on the Pacific. This project was never carried out. By the terms of the treaty the Government of Honduras guaranteed " that the inhabitants of the said islands should not be disturbed in the enjoyment of any property which they may have acquired therein, and should retain perfect freedom of religious belief and worship, public and private," &c., &c. I will now leave it to the reader to judge whether these terms have been fulfilled.

After twenty-five years of misrule, these unfortunate islanders are in a most pitiable plight; taxed to such a preposterous extent that it is scarcely possible for them to exist; their religion interfered with, inasmuch as they are not allowed to marry unless they go through a civil contract, thus becoming Honduranian subjects; their lands taken from them without a shadow of reason or justice; and if they complain, they are thrown into prison to await their trial, or are told to carry their complaints to H.B.M. consul at Truxillo, a seaport on the mainland. This functionary, a Jamaica Jew of Portuguese extraction, is married to a woman of the country, and is, moreover, in partnership with the President in business. It is not likely that the natives will get any redress from that quarter.

Failing this, they are told to go to Comayagua, the capital of the State, and lay their grievances there—an utter impossibility for an unfortunate negro, who does not even understand the language of the country.

Should their case be referred to H.M. Minister at Guatemala, a city far removed from the Atlantic coast, it is referred back to the consul at Truxillo. In despair of getting any redress, these unfortunate people eagerly swarm on board a man-of-war, feeling sure of a sympathetic hearing from the captain.

But the captains of H.M. ships are ordered not to listen to their complaints. The poor folk, failing to get justice from any quarter, at last petitioned Mr Barlee, our late Governor of British Honduras, for leave to settle once more on British soil.

Mr Barlee warmly espoused their cause, and arrangements were made for the purchase of land in the immediate neighbourhood of Belize; and an extensive exodus has already taken place from the islands to British Honduras. This appears to be the only solution of a difficult question; but it is hard for these people, who have raised the Bay Islands to their present prosperous state, to be driven from their homes, and told to begin life anew—especially as no compensation is given them for the property they leave behind. Lest I may be accused of exaggerating the facts, I may mention that, in conversation with the Governor of British Honduras on this subject, his Excellency remarked to me, "In no part of her Majesty's dominions are British subjects so shamefully ill-treated as are the Bay Islanders." It is idle to argue that they ought to have migrated at the time the islands were ceded, and that not having done so, they must take the consequences. This is the line taken by cold-blooded politicians. How could they have done so without ruin to themselves and their families?

As well might landed proprietors in this country be told to clear out, and seek a living elsewhere, leaving their property behind them, and receiving no compensation for it. In the extremely improbable event of this country being annexed by a foreign Power, they would have to do this, or become subjects of the conquerors!

Routan (pronounced *Ruatan*) is even more fertile than Bonacca, and the venomous flies which infest the latter do not exist here. The island is well populated, and is mostly under cultivation. All kinds of tropical fruits are to be found in profusion: the land is also suitable for coffee, cocoa, and tobacco, but the inhabitants being ground down by over-taxation, have no spirit left, and are only longing for the time when they can leave the island. Out of a population of over 5000, nine-tenths are British subjects, speaking only English—at least they consider themselves British subjects. The question seems to be, Does long residence in a foreign State make them subjects of that State; and if so, how long?

Some of the old inhabitants came to see me with tears in their eyes, bringing me the title-deeds to their land, signed, as they proudly showed, by her most gracious Majesty Queen Victoria. They stood on the quarter-deck, with their hats off, begging me to intercede for them, and asking that their lands might not be taken away.

"They were loyal subjects of her Majesty," they said; "and was not *her* signature a guarantee that they should not be molested?"

It was a humiliating thing to be obliged to confess that, although I sympathised deeply with them, I feared nothing could be done—that I felt sure her Majesty would feel for them if she knew the circumstances; but that as the island no longer belonged to her, she was powerless in the matter, and that my advice was to leave the country and place themselves once more under British protection. I told them I was going direct to Belize, and would give any of them a passage with pleasure, and would put their case before Mr Barlee, the Governor—and with this poor consolation they had to be content; but they all seemed grateful for a few kindly words and a little sympathy.

One poor old white-headed negro sat on the steps of the ladder leading from the gangway to the quarter-deck during our morning service, taking particular notice of the prayers, and humbly bowing his head at the conclusion. I sent for him and asked him what he wanted. He told me that twelve years ago his land had been taken away from him without cause, and he was left to starve. If the British Parliament only knew it, he would have justice, he exclaimed. I told the poor old fellow that it all happened so long ago, I feared the British Parliament could not help him even if they were inclined; and I advised him not to trust to that, but to endeavour to reconcile himself to his loss, and end his days in peace. I fear that the only land he will ever get out of those grasping wretches is six feet to lay his poor old bones in; and it will be a higher appeal than the British Parliament who will decide on the merits on his case: it is not likely he will have to wait long, either, for the verdict.

The Governor of Routan, Dobrucho Hernandez, a Honduranian Indian, rules these unfortunate people with a rod of iron, untempered with either justice, mercy, or common-sense. He resides in the town with a few other Government officials, and six officers and thirty soldiers, who form the garrison.

I waited on this individual to endeavour to ameliorate the condition of the negroes; but it is not likely anything will be done to improve their position.

It is true that the tax has been taken off the principal articles of food—such as flour, pork, and rice—simply because the poor people were unable to pay it, and were reduced to the verge of starvation.

The export tax on fruit has also been withdrawn; but other items, such as sugar, coffee, salt, soap, articles of clothing, and agricultural implements, are still charged from 50 to 100 per cent. In this way 60,000 dollars are annually raised, not one cent of which is spent upon the islands, or for the benefit of the inhabitants. I left Routan with bitter shame and regret—regret that I was unable to be of the slightest use to these unhappy folk, and ashamed that such beautiful islands should have been given up to their present possessors. A fair breeze carried us across to Belize in twenty-four hours.

I have already in a former chapter given a short description of Belize, so I have but few remarks to make on our present visit. I was told that some wonderful caves were to be seen about twenty miles to the southward, in which panthers were to be found, and that eyeless fish existed in a river in the caves; also, that the land in that neighbourhood was wonderfully rich, and suited for emigrants: so I made an expedition to the place, and having been nearly capsized on the bar at the entrance to the Manati river, found the spot.

The caves were a fraud, the panthers were not at home, and the river with the eyeless fish did not exist; but the trip was most enjoyable, and gave one the opportunity of seeing some fine country and beautiful scenery, combined with an agreeable climate. In this region most excellent land can be obtained at one dollar an acre; the soil is capable of producing sugar, tobacco, cocoa, and fruit of all kinds. Labour is scarce, and a labourer can earn six shillings a-day; consequently, for people of a humble class, this part of the country presents a favourable field for emigration. It is here that the unfortunate Bay Islanders may find a home.

A curious difficulty has lately arisen, owing to the cemeteries being overcrowded, and the impossibility of finding more land near Belize in which to bury the dead. Water is reached at a depth of two feet, so that a coffin has to be ballasted with stones to keep it down, and earth brought from a distance to cover it. To meet this difficulty the Governor caused vaults to be built above-ground; but the negro population, especially the women, opposed the measure with great bitterness, threatening to burn down the town if the obnoxious order was not recalled. Occasional scares take place in Belize, owing to the presence of hostile bands of Indians in the interior; but it is not considered probable that they will give trouble; and even if they do, I have no doubt the black troops will be equal to the occasion.

On our passage back to Jamaica, we touched at the Grand Cayman island, about which there is not very much to relate.

The island contains over 3000 inhabitants, who are mostly engaged in agriculture and the turtle trade. The turtle are brought from the Mosquito Coast, and transhipped to Jamaica. What soil there is on the island is of good quality, and produces fine crops of yams, cocoa (a vegetable somewhat resembling potato), Indian corn, bananas, pumpkins, plantains, melons, papaw, oranges, and limes. There is good pasturage for cattle, and over 1000 head are usually kept.

The island is healthy, and there is no resident doctor. The people say they get on very well without either doctors or lawyers; and I don't suppose a doctor would make a living. Nevertheless, considering the number of residents, one would suppose a doctor was needed. Possibly an individual combining the double duties of doctor and commissioner would be desirable. Some very fair craft are built at George Town, the capital, the woods of the country being used in their construction.

Very beautiful pink pearls are occasionally found in the conch-shells on the coast. These pearls are formed in the same manner as the oyster-pearl: they are of an oblong shape, and of a lovely rose-colour. The price varies from five to ten dollars; but some specimens are worth a great deal more.

From Grand Cayman we returned to Jamaica, and anchored in the beautiful harbour of Ocho Rios (eight rivers). Fair winds and fine weather, with a perfect temperature, had been our lot wherever we went; and if ever there was romance in connection with the sea, we certainly enjoyed it.

CHAPTER XVII.

SECOND VISIT TO HAÏTI, AND CONCLUSION.

WE had hardly swung round our buoy in Port Royal harbour a dozen times, or had time for more than a flying visit to our friends in the country, before alarming telegrams came from Mr Hunt, our acting consul-general at Port au Prince, detailing certain outrages which had been perpetrated upon foreigners by the Haïtien authorities. The presence of a man-of-war was urgently needed; so the Druid was ordered to proceed immediately to Haïti to put things straight.

Our first visit was to Miragoāne, a small port on the west coast of Haïti, where a disturbance had taken place. I found things a good deal "mixed" here. Mr Ahrendts, a German subject, but vice-consul for Great Britain, had been insulted, and thrown into prison. Mr Hadleigh, an American subject, had been served the same way. Mr Bain, a Scotchman in business in Port au Prince, was also in prison at that place, awaiting his trial on frivolous charges. It is a curious fact that, in whatever part of the world I have been in, I have always found a German, a Yankee, and a Scotchman, generally doing well. Here they were all represented; but they were in a tight place now.

Having embarked Messrs Ahrendts and Hadleigh at Miragoāne, we proceeded to Port au Prince, and communicated with Mr Hunt, after saluting the Haïtien flag with twenty-one guns.

We found things a good deal more "mixed" here: the Haïtien authorities seemed to have been perfectly impartial in the distribution of their favours. A French gentleman had been imprisoned illegally; two English gentlemen, staying with our consul, were unable to leave the house for fear of being seized and thrown into prison for some imaginary offence. The consul's house was watched by hired ruffians; ladies and gentlemen were insulted in the streets; and

British subjects imprisoned without cause. In fact, the Haïtien authorities had been having a high time of it in the absence of an English man-of-war. Mr Hunt assured me that he could obtain no redress or satisfaction: his earnest protestations were treated with contempt. He therefore placed the matter in my hands, to take what steps I thought proper.

There was no time to be lost. The poor Scotchman had been in prison three weeks, and three weeks in a Haïtien jail is no joke, with the thermometer at 120°, bad food, and most filthy quarters. The Haïtiens are a very polite nation, and their letters are invariably couched in the most courteous terms — in fact, they are adepts at the art of evasion. Under the circumstances, I was constrained to write very firmly, but politely, to his Excellency the President of the Republic, demanding the immediate release of Mr Bain, the Scotch gentleman, and that he be compensated for his incarceration of three weeks at the rate of 100 dollars (£20) per day for the whole time; also, that Mr Ahrendts, our vice-consul, who had been in prison five days, be awarded 1000 dollars; and Mr Hadleigh, 500 dollars; that the British flag be saluted, and an apology be tendered for the insult offered to it in the person of Mr Ahrendts; that the French gentleman be immediately released, and an apology tendered, no money compensation being desired in this case. Also, that the officials who committed these outrages should be dismissed from their posts, and that the nuisances complained of by H.M. consul, in respect to the precincts of his house being invaded by a lawless rabble, should immediately cease. These communications, which necessarily occupied some little time, and were spread over several letters, produced evasive replies, in order to gain time. I was ordered to use no force, but only persuasive measures, so no apparent preparation was visible on board the Druid. Her broadside was, however, within convenient range of the principal fort; and the first lieutenant was detailed to cut out a Haïtien man-of-war, by first breaking her cable with gun-cotton, and then towing her out under the guns of the Druid.

Fortunately diplomacy succeeded; and after

an interchange of numerous despatches, the Haïtien authorities agreed to these terms, with the exception of saluting the British flag on the Champs de Mars. This they begged to be excused from doing, as, they said, a rising of the people, and massacre of the whites, would be the probable result, together with the overthrow of the President. As our object was not to humiliate the nation, but to obtain satisfaction for the insults offered, I gladly waived this point, and the matter was at an end.

I paid an official visit to his Excellency the President, which was returned; and in forty-eight hours from the time the Druid anchored in the roads, the following results were obtained:—

1. An apology tendered for insults offered to the British flag, and dismissal of the Juge de Paix at Miragoāne.

2. One thousand dollars paid to Mr Ahrendts, and five hundred to Mr Hadleigh.

3. Mr Bain, British subject, released from prison, and paid two thousand dollars' compensation.

4. A French subject released from prison.

5. British subjects wrongfully imprisoned

and beaten at San Marks, released, and officials punished; compensation to be awarded.

6. Annoyance to Mr Hunt and his family removed.

7. Protection to British subjects and property guaranteed.

Before leaving Port au Prince, the foreign consuls and *chargés d'affaires* expressed to me their great satisfaction at the results obtained by the visit of H.M.S. Druid, and intimated their intention of making the same known to their respective Governments. Having seen the cash paid over the counter of the British consulate, and said good-bye to our friends, we returned to Jamaica.

On our arrival we learnt, to our intense disgust, that we were to proceed to Barbadoes.

Only those who have been away from home for three years and a half can appreciate our feelings on receipt of this news. Our spirits, buoyed up with the prospect of returning home at no distant period, now sank to zero.

We bade a sorrowful farewell to our friends, and prepared for our departure, when, on the 6th July, the joyful intelligence was received that we were to return to England, and on the 9th we sailed. A quick and pleasant passage took us to Bermuda, and on the 20th July we left it for the last time.

Our usual good fortune attended us across the Atlantic; and exactly one month after leaving Port Royal we sighted the shores of Old England.

After touching at Plymouth, we proceeded to Sheerness to pay off; and we had the gratification, so dear to a naval officer, of receiving the high approval of the Commander-in-Chief for the creditable state of the ship, together with a flattering letter from their lordships on paying off.

Appended is a list of ports touched at by the Druid during her commission, with the date of arrival and departure.

1879.

Place.	Arrival.		Departure.	
Commissioned at Sheerness	Feb.	18	Mar.	12
Plymouth	Mar.	14	"	18
Madeira	"	25	"	29
Bermuda	April	26	May	7
Halifax, N.S.	May	12	"	15
St John's, Newfoundland	"	19	June	5
Catalina	June	5	"	7
Harbour Grace	"	7	"	8
St John's	"	8	"	13
Trepassey	"	13	"	16
St Mary's	"	16	"	17
Salmonier	"	17	"	23
Colinet	"	23	"	24
Great St Lawrence	"	25	"	26
Harbour Briton	"	26	"	27
East Bay, Despair Bay	"	27	July	2
North Bay, Despair Bay	July	2	"	5
Hare Bay	"	5	"	6
Rencontre	"	6	"	7
La Poile	"	7	"	11
Port-au-Basque	"	11	"	12
St George's	"	13	"	15
Birchey Cove	"	15	"	18
Goose Bay	"	18	"	19
York Harbour	"	19	"	21
Bonne Bay	"	21	"	24
Port Saunders, Hawke's Bay	"	24	"	27
La Choix	"	27	"	27
Forteau	"	27	Aug.	4
Croque	Aug.	4	"	6
Paquet	"	6	"	6
St John's	"	9	"	29
Gready	Sept.	1	Sept.	2
Rigolet	"	2	"	3
Turner's Cove	"	3	"	4
Cartwright	"	4	"	6
St John's	"	9	"	19
La Poile	"	21	"	23
St George's	"	24	"	25, 26
Birchey Cove	"	27	Oct.	1
York Harbour	Oct.	1	"	4
Birchey Cove	"	4	"	16
La Poile	"	17	"	17
Salmonier	"	18	"	19
St John's	"	20	"	23
Halifax, N.S.	"	28	Nov.	13
Bermuda	Nov.	18	Dec.	4
Port Royal	Dec.	13	...	

1880.

Place.	Arrival.	Departure.
Port Royal	...	Jan. 7
Port Antonio	Jan. 8	" 21
Port Royal	" 21	" 26
Belize	" 30	Feb. 16
Havana	Feb. 19	" 23
Nuevitas	" 25	" 26
Guantanamo	" 28	" 29
Port Royal	Mar. 1	Mar. 15
Carthagena	" 18	" 26
Port Antonio	April 10	April 13
Port Royal	" 14	" 23
Bermuda	" 30	May 7
St John's	May 15	June 20
Harbour Grace	June 20	" 22
Trinity	" 22	" 25
Goose Bay	" 26	" 28
Clode Sound	" 28	" 29
Newman's Sound	" 29	" 30
Middle Arm, Bloody Bay	" 30	July 1
Freshwater Bay	July 1	" 2
Greenspond	" 2	" 3
Seldom-come-by	" 3	" 5
Gander River	" 5	" 6
Twillingate	" 6	" 8
Hall's Bay, Salmon River	" 8	" 12
Hall's Bay, Indian River	" 12	" 14
Paquet	" 14	" 15
Rouge	" 15	" 16
Croque	" 16	" 20
Hare Bay	" 20	" 21
St Anthony	" 21	" 24
Kirpon	" 24	" 25
Forteau	" 25	" 29
Loup Bay	" 29	" 29
St Barbe's	" 29	" 30
Hawke's Bay	" 30	Aug. 2
Bonne Bay	Aug. 2	" 7
Bay of Islands	" 7	" 10
La Poile	" 11	" 13
Little River	" 13	" 14
Hare Bay	" 14	" 15
Salmonier	" 16	" 19
Great Island	" 20	" 20
St John's	" 21	" 22

Place.	Arrival.	Departure.
Bay Bulls	Aug. 22	Aug. 23
Great Island	" 23	" 23
St John's	" 24	" 29
Great Island	" 29	" 29
St John's	" 29	Sept. 7
Great Island	Sept. 7	" 7
St John's	" 7	" 10
Great Island	" 10	" 10
Bay Bulls	" 10	" 10
St John's	" 10	" 12
Trepassey	" 12	" 14
St Mary's	" 14	" 15
Great St Lawrence	" 15	" 17
St Pierre	" 17	" 18
Ship Cove	" 18	" 21
Hare Bay	" 21	" 23
White Bear Bay	" 23	" 25
Bay of Islands	" 27	Oct. 2
York Harbour	Oct. 2	" 9
Lark Harbour	" 9	" 11
Bay of Islands	" 11	" 13
Sydney	" 14	" 15
St John's	" 18	" 29
Bermuda	Nov. 6	Dec. 4
Port Royal	Dec. 15	...

1881.

Place.	Arrival.	Departure.
Port Royal	...	Jan. 5
Port au Prince	Jan. 7	" 11
San Marks	" 11	" 12
Gonaives	" 12	" 14
Cape Haytien	" 15	" 17
Porto Plata	" 18	" 19
Samaná	" 20	" 21
San Domingo	" 23	" 24
Jacmel	" 26	" 27
Aux Cayes	" 28	" 29
Port Royal	" 30	Feb. 2
Montego Bay	Feb. 3	" 8
Port Royal	" 9	" 28
Port Royal	Mar. 4	Mar. 21
Havana	" 27	" 29
Bermuda	April 5	April 14
Halifax, N.S.	" 18	" 21
St Pierre	" 23	" 25

LIST OF PORTS TOUCHED AT

Place.	Arrival.	Departure.
Harbour Briton	April 25	April 26
St Jaques	" 26	" 27
Bellorum	" 27	" 27
Long Harbour	" 27	" 30
Tickle Beach	" 30	" 30
Bellorum	" 30	May 2
Great St Lawrence	May 2	" 3
Burin	" 3	" 4
Placentia	" 4	" 6
Salmonier	" 6	" 14
St Mary's	" 14	" 15
Trepassey	" 15	" 16
St John's	" 16	June 2
Harbour Grace	June 2	" 6
Heart's Content	" 6	" 7
Smith's Sound	" 7	" 9
Trinity	" 9	" 10
Twillingate	" 11	" 13
Burnt Arm, Exploit Bay	" 13	" 16
Peter's Arm, Exploit Bay	" 16	" 17
Hall's Bay	" 17	" 22
Little Bay	" 22	" 24
Robert's Arm	" 24	" 27
Little Bay	" 27	" 27
Middle Arm, Green Bay	" 27	" 28
Paquet	" 28	" 29
Croque	" 29	July 1
Hare Bay	July 1	" 3
St Anthony	" 3	" 4
Pistolet	" 4	" 5
Bonne Bay	" 6	" 8
Port Saunders	" 8	" 11
Hawke's Bay	" 11	" 12
St George's	" 13	" 15
Cod Roy	" 15	" 17
Cod Roy	" 18	" 19
Port-au-Basque	" 19	" 21
Sydney	" 21	" 25
Long Harbour, Fortune Bay	" 27	Aug. 3
Storey Harbour, Fortune Bay	Aug. 3	" 5
Harbour Briton	" 5	" 8
Halifax	" 11	" 17
Port-au-Basque	" 20	" 24
La Poile	" 24	" 26
Little River	" 26	" 27
Hare Bay	" 27	" 28
Bay du Nord	" 28	Sept. 3

Place.	Arrival.	Departure.
Ship Cove	Sept. 3	Sept. 6
St John's	" 6	" 26
Greenspond	" 27	" 28
Robert's Arm	" 30	Oct. 10
Hall's Bay	Oct. 10	" 12
Robert's Arm	" 12	" 12
Kirpon	" 15	" 17
St Anthony	" 17	" 17
St John's	" 19	" 22
Halifax	" 28	Nov. 1
Bermuda	Nov. 8	Dec. 14
Port Royal	Dec. 24	...

1882.

Place.	Arrival.	Departure.
Port Royal	...	Jan. 6
Havana	Jan. 12	" 17
Matanzas	" 17	" 19
Cay Sal	" 20	" 21
Cay Anguilla	" 21	" 21
Nipé	" 24	" 26
Inagua	" 28	" 30
Port Antonio	Feb. 1	Feb. 6
Port Royal	" 6	" 27
Lucea	Mar. 3	Mar. 6
Port Royal	" 7	" 27
Port Antonio	" 28	April 3
Port Royal	April 3	" 13
Inagua	" 14	" 18
Port Royal	" 19	" 29
Old Providence	May 3	May 6
Swan Islands	" 8	" 10
Bonacca	" 11	" 15
Routan	" 15	" 16
Belize	" 17	" 25
Grand Cayman	" 29	" 30
Montego Bay	June 1	June 1
Ocho Rios	" 2	" 7
Port Royal	" 8	" 19
Miragoâne	" 21	" 22
Port au Prince	" 22	" 29
Port Roya	July 1	July 9
Bermuda	" 17	" 20
Plymouth	Aug. 10	Aug. 11
Sheerness	" 13	...

PRINTED BY WILLIAM BLACKWOOD AND SONS.

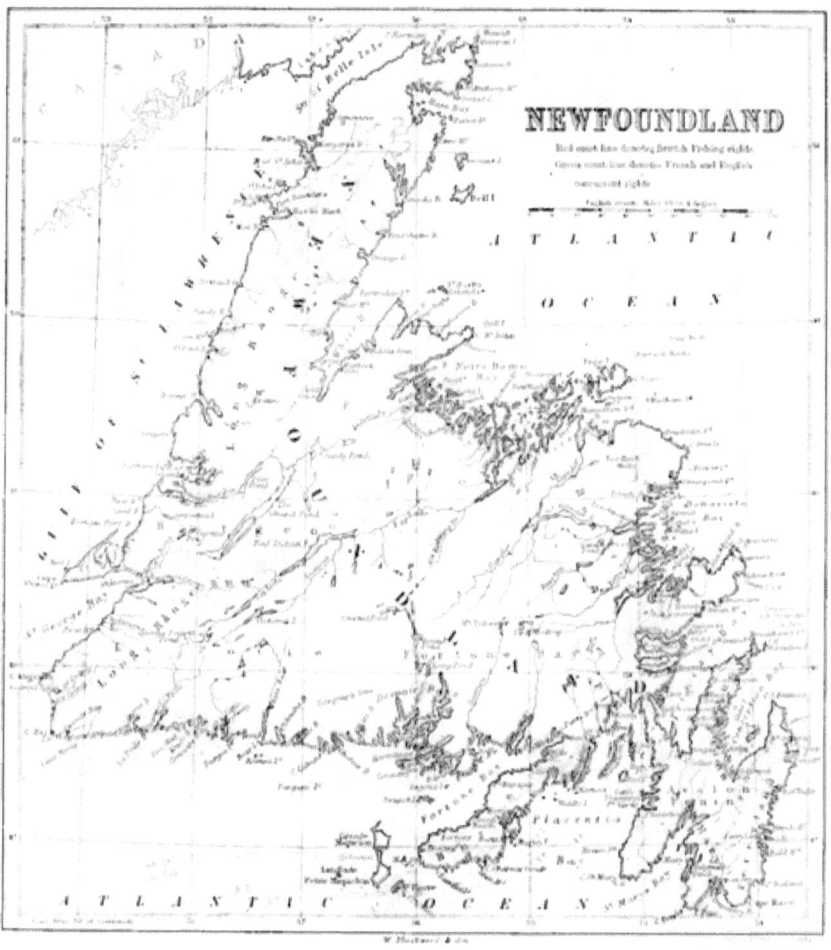

www.ingramcontent.com/pod-product-compliance
Lightning Source LLC
Chambersburg PA
CBHW022110290426
44112CB00008B/614